VOLUME 2

OLD TESTAMENT

THE NEW COLLEGEVILLE BIBLE COMMENTARY

GENESIS

Joan E. Cook, S.C.

SERIES EDITOR

Daniel Durken, O.S.B.

LITURGICAL PRESS
Collegeville, Minnesota

www.litpress.org

Nihil obstat: Reverend Robert C. Harren, *Censor deputatus.*
Imprimatur: ✠ Most Reverend John F. Kinney, Bishop of St. Cloud, Minnesota, December 17, 2010.

Design by Ann Blattner.

Cover illustration: Creation detail from *Creation, Covenant, Shekinah, Kingdom* by Donald Jackson. Copyright 2006 *The Saint John's Bible,* Order of Saint Benedict, Collegeville, Minnesota USA. Used by permission. All rights reserved.

Photos: pages 12, 34, 92, 138, Photos.com; page 26, Wikimedia Commons.

	5	6	7	8	9

Library of Congress Cataloging-in-Publication Data

Cook, Joan E.
    Genesis / Joan E. Cook.
        p.   cm. — (The new Collegeville Bible commentary. Old Testament ; v. 2)
    ISBN 978-0-8146-2836-2
        1. Bible. O.T. Genesis—Commentaries.   I. Title.

    BS1235.53.C66 2010
    222'.1107—dc22

                                                                2009039373

CONTENTS

ABBREVIATIONS

Books of the Bible

Acts—Acts of the Apostles
Amos—Amos
Bar—Baruch
1 Chr—1 Chronicles
2 Chr—2 Chronicles
Col—Colossians
1 Cor—1 Corinthians
2 Cor—2 Corinthians
Dan—Daniel
Deut—Deuteronomy
Eccl (or Qoh)—Ecclesiastes
Eph—Ephesians
Esth—Esther
Exod—Exodus
Ezek—Ezekiel
Ezra—Ezra
Gal—Galatians
Gen—Genesis
Hab—Habakkuk
Hag—Haggai
Heb—Hebrews
Hos—Hosea
Isa—Isaiah
Jas—James
Jdt—Judith
Jer—Jeremiah
Job—Job
Joel—Joel
John—John
1 John—1 John
2 John—2 John
3 John—3 John
Jonah—Jonah
Josh—Joshua
Jude—Jude
Judg—Judges
1 Kgs—1 Kings

2 Kgs—2 Kings
Lam—Lamentations
Lev—Leviticus
Luke—Luke
1 Macc—1 Maccabees
2 Macc—2 Maccabees
Mal—Malachi
Mark—Mark
Matt—Matthew
Mic—Micah
Nah—Nahum
Neh—Nehemiah
Num—Numbers
Obad—Obadiah
1 Pet—1 Peter
2 Pet—2 Peter
Phil—Philippians
Phlm—Philemon
Prov—Proverbs
Ps(s)—Psalms
Rev—Revelation
Rom—Romans
Ruth—Ruth
1 Sam—1 Samuel
2 Sam—2 Samuel
Sir—Sirach
Song—Song of Songs
1 Thess—1 Thessalonians
2 Thess—2 Thessalonians
1 Tim—1 Timothy
2 Tim—2 Timothy
Titus—Titus
Tob—Tobit
Wis—Wisdom
Zech—Zechariah
Zeph—Zephaniah

The Book of Genesis

Genesis is a story about beginnings: of the universe, of humans, of joys and sorrows, successes and failures. The book focuses on the relationships between God and people as well as those among different people. These themes are simple in principle, but often complex in our lives. While the themes of Genesis are universal they can be complex because they are expressed in the styles and settings of the ancient Near East. Before we look at the book itself, several introductory points will facilitate our reading of Genesis.

Themes

Genesis introduces several themes that permeate the entire Bible. The first of these is divine causality; that is, the ancient people believed that the deities caused everything that happened in life. The ancient Israelites came to believe in only one God, whose name they eventually learned was Lord or "I AM" (Exod 3:14). They believed that the one God who caused everything to happen took a special interest in them. This divine-human relationship was understood as essential, and it applied not only to the relationship between God and the people, but also among people.

An implication of the importance of relationships is the setting of boundaries between God and creatures, including human beings, and between different creatures. The boundaries involved right relationships among all creatures and also between humans and God. In addition, boundaries factored into the topic of land and the possession of land. Finally, intimately connected to the theme of relationship is the theme of promise and blessing. The Creator promises to remember and care for all creation, and carries out that promise in spite of the many ways that creatures violate divinely set boundaries.

Ancient storytelling

Another important topic is the way in which ancient people expressed their beliefs and values and told their story: it is quite different from the way we today record our past. We strive to record information with great attention to the details of the event, such as when and where it took place, who was involved, what they did and said. Then we use these details in our efforts to interpret the event we record. But in the ancient world, the project of remembering the past took a different form. People were not as concerned with recording the precise details of an event as they were in probing its meaning. To that end they told stories.

This means of communication was ideally suited to nonliterate cultures, peoples who depended on oral communication because very few could read and write. The stories they told embodied the larger meanings they found in situations and events, and related them in ways their listeners would remember and pass down to their descendants. In fact, we will note throughout Genesis that some events were recounted more than once, with different points of focus and emphasis. The variations were included because each one added to the meaning of the event, and to the overall picture of the people's relationship with one another and with their God.

Ancient Near Eastern parallels

Several Genesis stories have parallels in other ancient Near Eastern cultures. The best-known of these are the Mesopotamian creation myth called *Enuma Elish*, of which echoes can be seen in the Genesis creation stories, and a Mesopotamian myth about the quest for immortality called the Epic of Gilgamesh, of which traces are evident in the Genesis flood story. Other parts of Genesis include what appear to be allusions to ancient stories. The parallel stories provide plots and themes onto which the Genesis narratives superimposed the ancient Israelites' beliefs. We will comment on *Enuma Elish* and the Epic of Gilgamesh in our discussion of the biblical creation and flood stories.

Documentary hypothesis

As the ancient Near Eastern people continued to tell their stories throughout the generations, the stories took on characteristic themes and motifs typical of their particular geographical localities and political and socioeconomic situations. When the people eventually began to write down their stories, these particularities became part of the narrative. The process of recording the material was a complex one that extended over hundreds of years. In the past 150 years, scholars have studied this question and have developed a theory as to how the first five books of the Bible (also known as the Pentateuch, which includes the book of Genesis) developed into the form we have today. That theory is known as the Documentary Hypothesis. We will look at the contemporary understanding of this theory with regard to the book of Genesis, because an understanding of how the book probably came into its present form is helpful to an understanding of the book's content.

According to the theory, the process of setting the stories in writing took place over a period of several hundred years, from about 1000 B.C. to about 500 B.C. Before that the stories circulated by word of mouth in families and clans. Then around 1000 B.C. when David was King of Israel, he took steps to unite the twelve tribes into one people. One of those steps was to commission his scribes to write down the people's stories, weaving them into one. This early strand of Genesis (in fact, of the entire Pentateuch) is called J to represent the German spelling of the word Yahweh (Jahweh), the name by which this strand of the Pentateuch refers to God.

After King Solomon's death about one hundred years later, the kingdom David had established broke into two: the northern and southern kingdoms. The southern kingdom, Judah, believed it was the one that remained loyal to God and to the divine promises. The northern kingdom, Israel, set about establishing a new identity, and one of its steps was to rewrite parts of the early J story, inserting new details and substituting different names according to their own regional usage. This strand was woven into the earlier story, and the new strand became known as E because it calls God Elohim.

About five hundred years later, the city of Jerusalem and the entire southern kingdom of Judah endured a traumatic defeat by the Babylonians. They destroyed the temple, which had become the central place of worship. They also imprisoned the king and took into exile many leading members of the Jerusalem community. This defeat represented not only a political act but also the violation of the divine promises that had sustained the people since the time of Abraham and Sarah, over one thousand years before. The upheaval caused the people to rethink the beliefs that had sustained them throughout those one thousand years. The result was two additional strands. The first is known as D and represents the efforts of the people to understand their exile in terms of the message of the book of Deuteronomy: reliance on the covenant, or the formal terms of the relationship between God and the people. The D writers understood the exile as punishment for their own violation of the terms God had set down for the people. They believed that the exile was not a failure of the deity to keep the divine promises, but rather the failure of the people to live up to them.

Finally, a group of priests, also working to understand the meaning of the exile, preserved a record of how they had practiced their religion when it was centered in the Jerusalem temple. They did this because they saw the temple worship as the norm for public practice of religion. They wanted to preserve this record in the hope that one day they would return to Jerusalem, rebuild the temple, and resume temple worship according to the record they left for future generations. And if the exile did not end, at least there would be a record of how religion was practiced in the "good old days" of temple-centered religion. This strand is called P for the priestly authors who are believed to have written it. These last two groups, D and P, were probably not simply writers but also editors, who worked their strands into the earlier ones and gave the entire Pentateuch the shape we know today.

This summary gives an idea of the stages in the writing of Genesis. We can also categorize the four strands in terms of their characteristic features. We have seen that the writers and editors used different names for the deity: the Yahwist, or J, used the term YHWH, the name God gave to Moses at the burning bush in response to Moses' request in Exodus 3:13-14. The Elohist, on the other hand, used the name Elohim, a term that originally meant "gods" and that ancient Israel used in referring to their own God. A shortened form of the word is "El," another term we find in Genesis. The editors we call P also used the term Elohim to refer to the deity.

The four sources have other characteristics, too. The J strand is the storytelling piece, with details that enable us to see, hear, and feel the events described in that strand of the narrative. Its descriptions of the deity are vivid and concrete: they describe God in ways that we humans can identify with, as we will see in Genesis 2. On the other hand, the E strand tends to focus on the transcendence of God, describing the divine presence in dreams and other ways that highlight the mysterious quality of divine presence and action. The D strand tends to be solemn and formal, and to emphasize the cause-and-effect quality of human actions while at the same time recognizing divine inbreakings in unexpected and surprising ways. Finally, the P strand focuses on concerns relating to the public practice of religion: the details of rituals, the place of different people within society, the relationships among different people that are often expressed in genealogical lists. Genesis is composed primarily of the J and P strands; we will point them out in the places where it enhances our understanding of the story.

Ancient literary genres

Another element to consider in our reading of the book of Genesis is the ancient genres or types of writings that comprise the book. The people spoke and wrote according to the conventions of the day. There are three main types of writing that appear frequently in Genesis: myths, sagas, and genealogies. The first two are narrative forms. Myths, in the biblical sense, are not make-believe stories. Rather, they are stories that convey the beliefs and values of the people. We will get a better idea of what this means when we look at the myths in the book. The other narrative genre, the saga, is a story that tells about the past and relates it to the present. The Genesis sagas tell about the beginnings of the world and about events within families. Sagas are predominantly the work of J.

The genealogies appear throughout the book, enumerating the relationships among different generations. These lists are among the latest parts of the book, added during or toward the end of the exile in Babylon to produce a record of who belonged to the group of exiles from Judah. Such a record served several important purposes: it established the record of the family ties of different people, identifying how they belonged to the chosen people. In addition, it supported the claims to the land that became vitally important when the exiles returned to their land and needed to legitimate their claim to it, because others had settled there in their absence. The genealogical lists are the work of P, and they not only identify the relationships among the different people, they also provide an organizing principle for the book of Genesis. We will look at these lists and the information we can learn from them.

By taking note of the three genres—myths, saga, and genealogy—we can understand what the Second Vatican Council document on revelation, *Dei Verbum*, meant in referring to the Bible as the word of God in human language. We believe that the Bible is the word of God, that is, revelation from God. At the same time we believe that it is recorded by human beings who put down the information in the ways people communicated with one another at the time the words were put into writing, according to the genres of the day.

Keeping all these facets in mind—the overall themes of Genesis; the lengthy process of recording and editing that brought the book to the form in which we know it today; the characteristics of the four different strands J, E, D, and P; the literary forms in which the ancient writers and editors wrote their messages; and the ancient Near Eastern parallel literature— gives us useful tools for understanding the book of Genesis. Now let us look at the contents of the book.

Divisions of the book of Genesis

The Genesis story consists of three parts. The first is the Primeval Story, the story of the earliest beginnings of the universe and of human beings on earth. It is found in chapters 1–11 of Genesis. The second part is the Ancestral Story, the story of several generations who became the ancestors of God's people. They were Abraham and Sarah; Rebekah and Isaac; Jacob and his two wives Leah and Rachel, their maids Bilhah and Zilpah, and their twelve sons and one daughter. This part of the story is found in chapters 12–36. The final part of the Ancestral Story focuses on one of Jacob's sons, Joseph, and his adventures that resulted in the family of Jacob being given a privileged place in the land of Egypt. This part of the story is found in chapters 37–50. We will now begin our reading of the book, looking at each of these three sections and the stories in each in some detail.

As we read, we will keep in mind that we are looking simultaneously at two different historical periods: the time described and the time when the story was written down. The way in which each historical, or prehistoric, episode is recorded reflects not only the people's understanding of what happened but also the context in which they wrote: the political, economic, and religious concerns that were important at the time, and through which they found meaning in the ancient narrative.

The Book of Genesis

THE PRIMEVAL STORY

Genesis 1:1–11:28

The Primeval Story in Genesis 1–11 is the story of the earliest beginnings of the universe and of the human race. It talks of prehistoric times, naming a few places that we can identify today such as the Tigris and Euphrates Rivers, but for the most part it recounts stories whose details we cannot identify with precision; often we can find parallel stories and themes in other ancient Near Eastern myths. The Primeval Story consists of two creation stories, followed by several examples of humans who missed the mark in their efforts to live up to the ideals of creation. The best known are the stories of Adam, Eve, and the serpent; the murder of Abel by his brother Cain; the Flood; and the tower of Babel. Each of these stories invites us to look at life's challenges and how we respond to them as individuals and communities.

The Primeval Story takes us back to that primordial time when God created the world. Today we struggle to weigh different theories of how the universe came into being: whether by divine fiat, by evolution, by intelligent design, or by some other means that we do not yet understand. Ancient peoples also struggled to understand how the world came into being. They expressed their questions and theories in stories, rather than in the scientific theories we propose today. This difference is an important one to note when we read the Old Testament. Ancient peoples used stories to express their beliefs and values. These stories were not primarily concerned with relating the facts of a given situation; rather, they expressed the contemporary meaning their tellers found in ancient events and circumstances.

The first two chapters of Genesis tell two stories of how the world came into being. The two stories have several common elements: one Creator made the universe by shaping and organizing everything within the confines of time and space to make sure that every creature belonged in it and

մ զգում և նոր ուրախացագան ։ ՝ Գաբրիէլ հայրմat ։ ՝

Preamble.
The Creation of the World

◀ **1** **The Story of Creation.** [1]In the beginning, when God created the heavens ◀ and the earth—[2]and the earth was without form or shape, with darkness over the abyss and a mighty wind sweeping over the waters— *Day 1*

◀ [3]Then God said: Let there be light, ◀ and there was light. [4]God saw that the light was good. God then separated the light from the darkness. [5]God called the light "day," and the darkness he called "night." Evening came, and morning followed—the first day. *Day 2*

[6]Then God said: Let there be a dome in the middle of the waters, to separate one body of water from the other. [7]God made the dome, and it separated the water below the dome from the water above the dome. And so it happened. [8]God called the dome "sky." Evening

nothing was destroyed. Among all the creatures, humans were given a special place.

Each of the two stories has distinctive features as well. These give each story its unique character.

1:1–2:4a First creation story

Genesis 1:1–2:4a describes a seven-day process during which the Creator's word, "Let there be . . ." brings the different elements of the universe into being. The first three days witness the creation of the environment, and the second three days parallel the first, with the creation of creatures to live in the different spaces in the environment. We can chart this parallel in the following way:

Days 1-3	Days 4-6
Light, Day and Night	Greater Light, Lesser Light, Stars
Water and Sky	Fish and Birds
Land and Sea, Plants	Earth Creatures, Animal and Human

Creation begins with a powerful wind sweeping over the waters. Then the activity of each day begins with the formula, "God said: Let there be . . ." Then the narrative reports the specific activity for the day. At the end of the first, third, fourth, and sixth days, God saw that it was "good."

▶ This symbol indicates a cross reference number in the *Catechism of the Catholic Church*. See page 156 for number citations.

Adam and Eve expelled from the Garden of Eden. A 16th-century manuscript illumination from Armenia.

Day 3

came, and morning followed—the second day.

[9]Then God said: Let the water under the sky be gathered into a single basin, so that the dry land may appear. And so it happened: the water under the sky was gathered into its basin, and the dry land appeared. [10]God called the dry land "earth," and the basin of water he called "sea." God saw that it was good. [11]Then God said: Let the earth bring forth vegetation: every kind of plant that bears seed and every kind of fruit tree on earth that bears fruit with its seed in it. And so it happened: [12]the earth brought forth vegetation: every kind of plant that bears

seed and every kind of fruit tree that bears fruit with its seed in it. God saw that it was good. [13]Evening came, and morning followed—the third day.

Day 4

[14]Then God said: Let there be lights in the dome of the sky, to separate day from night. Let them mark the seasons, the days and the years, [15]and serve as lights in the dome of the sky, to illuminate the earth. And so it happened: [16]God made the two great lights, the greater one to govern the day, and the lesser one to govern the night, and the stars. [17]God set them in the dome of the sky, to illuminate the earth, [18]to govern the day and the night, and to separate the light from

On the sixth day, after all the creatures had been created, God looked over all of creation and saw that it was "very good" (1:31). The description of each day's work ends with the notation, "Evening came, and morning followed . . . ," then gives the number of the day. The account illustrates the power ancient people associated with the spoken word: to speak was to set an action in motion; thus speech had a sacramental quality insofar as it caused what it signified. The formulas suggest the unfolding of a ritual: creation occurs according to an organized plan by which God first creates the environment, then populates it with creatures suitable for that particular part of the universe.

In verse 6 the dome, or firmament, represents the ancient Near Eastern concept of a divider between the heavens and the earth. We can picture it as a large bowl inverted and set on a flat surface. Everything under the bowl is inside the firmament, and the rest is outside it.

One of the first acts of creation is to harness the waters by assigning them to specific places in the cosmos. This attention to water highlights its necessity for life, and the need to protect and preserve it in the arid ancient Near Eastern climate.

The separation of light from darkness in 1:14 makes it possible to count the passage of time, not only according to days but also to seasons and years. God blesses the creatures of the sea, air, and earth (v. 22), commanding them to be fertile and multiply, assuring the continuity of creation.

the darkness. God saw that it was good. [19]Evening came, and morning followed—the fourth day.

[20]Then God said: Let the water teem with an abundance of living creatures, and on the earth let birds fly beneath the dome of the sky. [21]God created the great sea monsters and all kinds of crawling living creatures with which the water teems, and all kinds of winged birds. God saw that it was good, [22]and God blessed them, saying: Be fertile, multiply, and fill the water of the seas; and let the birds multiply on the earth. [23]Evening came, and morning followed—the fifth day.

[24]Then God said: Let the earth bring forth every kind of living creature: tame animals, crawling things, and every kind of wild animal. And so it happened: [25]God made every kind of wild animal, every kind of tame animal, and every kind of thing that crawls on the ground. God saw that it was good. [26]Then God said: Let us make human beings in our image, after our likeness. Let them have dominion over the fish of the sea, the birds of the air, the tame animals, all the wild animals, and all the creatures that crawl on the earth.

[27]God created mankind in his
  image;
in the image of God he created
  them;
male and female he created
  them.

The Creator gives a special place to humanity in 1:26. Humans, male and female, are made in the image of God. This is a puzzling statement, for which several explanations have been suggested. For example, we were made with the ability to make decisions, just as God does; or we are the visible "image" of the invisible God in the world. As God's human counterpart, we have the ability to communicate with God and to ask "Why?" when we do not understand. We also have dominion over all the other creatures. This awesome responsibility involves nurturing and protecting all the other creatures in the universe. The biblical story contrasts with the Mesopotamian *Enuma Elish*, which is full of violence and oppression. In that version the gods compete for the opportunity to create the universe. The victor, Marduk, creates humans to serve the gods.

The seventh day is designated as holy because it is God's day of rest (2:3). In the ancient world "holy" meant "set aside for God." Legislation concerning sabbath observance relied on this model of divine rest. It gives us an example for how to spend the day of the week that is set aside for God. A summary statement marks the end of the first creation account.

This first creation account is the work of the P editor. At the time of its compilation the people of Jerusalem were in exile in Babylon as a result of the Babylonian takeover of the ancient Near East. They were searching for

15

◄ ²⁸God blessed them and God said to them: Be fertile and multiply; fill the earth and subdue it. Have dominion over the fish of the sea, the birds of the air, and all the living things that crawl on the earth. ²⁹God also said: See, I give you every seed-bearing plant on all the earth and every tree that has seed-bearing fruit on it to be your food; ³⁰and to all the wild animals, all the birds of the air, and all the living creatures that crawl on the earth, I give all the green plants for food.

◄ And so it happened. ³¹God looked at everything he had made, and found it very good. Evening came, and morning followed—the sixth day.

◄ **2** ¹Thus the heavens and the earth and
◄ all their array were completed. ²On the seventh day God completed the work he had been doing; he rested on the seventh day from all the work he had undertaken. ³God blessed the seventh day and made it holy, because on it he rested from all the work he had done in creation.

I. The Story of the Nations

The Garden of Eden. ⁴This is the story of the heavens and the earth at their creation. When the LORD God made the earth and the heavens—⁵there was no field shrub on earth and no grass of the field had sprouted, for the LORD God had sent no rain upon the earth and there was no man to till the ground, ⁶but a stream was welling up out of the earth and watering all the surface of the ground—⁷then the LORD God formed ►

---

the meaning of their exile, and for evidence that God still cared for them and maintained the universe. The insertion of the account, one of the last to be composed, at the beginning of the entire Bible introduces the themes of one God, divine concern for creatures, the dignity of human beings, and the orderly division of creation into different habitats for different creatures, different times for different activities, and the importance of honoring God in difficult times as well as moments of celebration.

2:4b-25 Second creation story

Immediately after the first story of creation, a second one follows. Like the first, it highlights the special place of humans in creation, relating it in a storytelling mode. We can picture the divine creative actions: shaping things out of clay, planting a garden, instructing the human on how to act in the garden. The breath of God suggests the same kind of energy found in the first creation story: the blowing wind is an invisible force that causes things to happen. God's first act of creation in this account is to shape a human being from the dust of the earth. Again we notice the importance of water: a stream waters all the ground, making it possible to work the soil, and becomes four rivers. Two of these rivers, the Tigris and Euphrates, run through Turkey, Syria, and Iraq.

the man out of the dust of the ground and blew into his nostrils the breath of life, and the man became a living being.

[8]The Lord God planted a garden in Eden, in the east, and placed there the man whom he had formed. [9]Out of the ground the Lord God made grow every tree that was delightful to look at and good for food, with the tree of life in the middle of the garden and the tree of the knowledge of good and evil.

[10]A river rises in Eden to water the garden; beyond there it divides and becomes four branches. [11]The name of the first is the Pishon; it is the one that winds through the whole land of Havilah, where there is gold. [12]The gold of that land is good; bdellium and lapis lazuli are also there. [13]The name of the second river is the Gihon; it is the one that winds all through the land of Cush. [14]The name of the third river is the Tigris; it is the one that flows east of Asshur. The fourth river is the Euphrates.

[15]The Lord God then took the man and settled him in the garden of Eden, to cultivate and care for it. [16]The Lord God gave the man this order: You are free to eat from any of the trees of the garden [17]except the tree of knowledge of good and evil. From that tree you shall not eat; when you eat from it you shall die.

[18]The Lord God said: It is not good for the man to be alone. I will make a helper suited to him. [19]So the Lord God

---

The prohibition in verse 17 not to eat from the tree of knowledge of good and evil carries with it the threat of death. Death is not explained here; its meaning is already known by the time the story is set in writing, probably around 1000 B.C. The mention of it foreshadows the snake's temptation of the humans in the next chapter, where punishment by death is best explained as an etiological detail, which is an explanation of one of life's realities.

This creation story highlights the importance of relationships: God makes all the other creatures in an effort to provide a suitable companion for the human (v. 18). Only another human can offer that companionship, which finds its ultimate expression in marriage. The solemn wording of verse 24, "That is why . . ." identifies this verse as another etiology, or explanation of the reality of marriage.

This second creation story is the work of J, the storyteller who first collated the ancient stories in an effort to establish a common memory for the tribes united under David. It depicts the work of creation by giving concrete details and describing God in immanent terms. In other words, it depicts God with descriptions that enable us to know God's nearness to us. We can contrast this description with that in the first creation story, which depicts God as transcendent, or far beyond our ability to comprehend. The

formed out of the ground all the wild animals and all the birds of the air, and he brought them to the man to see what he would call them; whatever the man called each living creature was then its name. ²⁰The man gave names to all the tame animals, all the birds of the air, and all the wild animals; but none proved to be a helper suited to the man.

²¹So the LORD God cast a deep sleep on the man, and while he was asleep, he took out one of his ribs and closed up its place with flesh. ²²The LORD God then built the rib that he had taken from the man into a woman. When he brought her to the man, ²³the man said:

"This one, at last, is bone of my bones
and flesh of my flesh;
This one shall be called 'woman,'
for out of man this one has been taken."

²⁴That is why a man leaves his father and mother and clings to his wife, and the two of them become one body.

²⁵The man and his wife were both naked, yet they felt no shame.

Expulsion from Eden. ¹Now the snake was the most cunning of all the wild animals that the LORD God had made. He asked the woman, "Did God really say, 'You shall not eat from any of

juxtaposition of the two stories illustrates the belief that God is both transcendent and immanent: infinitely beyond our ability to grasp and at the same time here in our midst.

After the two creation stories, the Primeval Story describes incidents in which humans begin to violate the boundaries the Creator has established between God and creatures. Each of the stories describes the way the boundary is violated, gives a divine declaration of that violation and the tendency to evil, and reports divine actions to restore the balance in the relationship between God and humans. Interwoven with these are etiological tales about place names, customs, or human realities; for example, marriage, the wearing of clothes, the reality of shame, evil, and death. At different points throughout the stories, genealogies name those who belong to the different tribes and clans and specify the relationships among them. The names are often eponymous: names of individuals become the names of groups such as Israel, the name given to Jacob in 32:29.

3:1-24 Adam, Eve, and the serpent

The creation story in chapter 2 includes the divine prohibition against eating the fruit of a particular tree that God gave to the first human before the creation of the woman. Here a new creature enters the picture, described only as a snake. No physical description is given until the creature receives the divine punishment for leading the humans into sin (vv. 14-15). At that

the trees in the garden'?" ²The woman answered the snake: "We may eat of the fruit of the trees in the garden; ³it is only about the fruit of the tree in the middle of the garden that God said, 'You shall not eat it or even touch it, or else you will die.'" ⁴But the snake said to the woman: "You certainly will not die! ⁵God knows well that when you eat of it your eyes will be opened and you will be like gods, who know good and evil." ⁶The woman saw that the tree was good for food and pleasing to the eyes, and the tree was desirable for gaining wisdom. So she took some of its fruit and ate it; and she also gave some to her husband, who was with her, and he ate it. ⁷Then the eyes of both of them were opened, and they knew that they were naked; so they sewed fig leaves together and made loincloths for themselves.

⁸When they heard the sound of the LORD God walking about in the garden at the breezy time of the day, the man and his wife hid themselves from the LORD God among the trees of the garden. ⁹The LORD God then called to the man and asked him: Where are you? ¹⁰He answered, "I heard you in the garden; but I was afraid, because I was naked, so I hid." ¹¹Then God asked: Who told you that you were naked? Have you eaten from the tree of which I had forbidden you to eat? ¹²The man replied, "The woman whom you put here with me— she gave me fruit from the tree, so I ate it." ¹³The LORD God then asked the woman: What is this you have done? The woman answered, "The snake tricked me, so I ate it."

¹⁴Then the LORD God said to the snake:

---

point the creature loses its legs and is condemned to crawl on the ground, eat dirt, and reach up only to the heels of humans. The creature is a tempter, but is not the devil in the modern sense of that term.

The snake approaches the woman while the man is with her (v. 6), misquoting the divine prohibition by applying it to all the fruit trees (v. 4). She in turn adds to the original prohibition the command not even to touch the forbidden fruit under pain of death (v. 3). The snake's words immediately characterize him as cunning, and the woman's words portray her as eager to observe the divine prohibition. The snake capitalizes on the reason for avoiding the fruit: death will follow. Even though death has not been explained, the story makes clear that the Creator, the snake, and the woman all see it as something to avoid. Here the story resembles other ancient Near Eastern myths that describe the futile efforts of creatures to become immortal. The snake then insinuates that the divine prohibition has a different motive: eating the fruit gives to humans divine knowledge of good and evil; eating the fruit will make the humans like gods.

This is a complex idea: God made the humans in the divine image; the temptation is to eat in order to become more like God by knowing as much

Because you have done this,
     cursed are you
     among all the animals, tame or
          wild;
On your belly you shall crawl,
     and dust you shall eat
     all the days of your life.
¹⁵I will put enmity between you and
          the woman,
     and between your offspring and
          hers;
They will strike at your head,
     while you strike at their heel.

¹⁶To the woman he said:

I will intensify your toil in child-
          bearing;
     in pain you shall bring forth
          children.
Yet your urge shall be for your
          husband,
     and he shall rule over you.

¹⁷To the man he said: Because you
listened to your wife and ate from the
tree about which I commanded you, You
shall not eat from it,

Cursed is the ground because of you!
     In toil you shall eat its yield
     all the days of your life.
¹⁸Thorns and thistles it shall bear
          for you,
     and you shall eat the grass of
          the field.
¹⁹By the sweat of your brow
     you shall eat bread,
Until you return to the ground,
     from which you were taken;
For you are dust,
     and to dust you shall return.

²⁰The man gave his wife the name
"Eve," because she was the mother of all
the living.

---

as God, ironically, about good and evil. The fruit promises to have more benefits than the snake first mentions: it tastes good, is beautiful, and gives wisdom. The woman eats some, then gives some to the man who does the same. As soon as they have eaten, the snake's promise proves true: they have increased knowledge that shows itself in their awareness of their nakedness. Ironically, the couple now know about good and evil through experience: they have taken it into themselves.

The divine question in verse 9, "Where are you?" underscores the tragic rupture of the divine-human relationship caused by human efforts to usurp divine power. The sin is thus in crossing the boundary that God set for them. They attempt to go beyond the limits of humanity and usurp power that belongs only to God.

The Lord God punishes all three: snake, woman, and man. Of the three, the words to the woman are the fewest, and she is not accused of committing the first sin. That idea does not appear in the Bible until Sirach 25:24: "With a woman sin had a beginning, / and because of her we all die." The punishments are etiologies that explain such human questions as "Why are women and men attracted to each other?" "Why do some people try to

²¹The Lord God made for the man and his wife garments of skin, with which he clothed them. ²²Then the Lord God said: See! The man has become like one of us, knowing good and evil! Now, what if he also reaches out his hand to take fruit from the tree of life, and eats of it and lives forever? ²³The Lord God therefore banished him from the garden of Eden, to till the ground from which he had been taken. ²⁴He expelled the man, stationing the cherubim and the fiery revolving sword east of the garden of Eden, to guard the way to the tree of life.

Cain and Abel. ¹The man had intercourse with his wife Eve, and she conceived and gave birth to Cain, saying, "I have produced a male child with the help of the Lord." ²Next she gave birth to his brother Abel. Abel became a herder of flocks, and Cain a tiller of the ground. ³In the course of time Cain brought an offering to the Lord from the fruit of the ground, ⁴while Abel, for his part, brought the fatty portion of the firstlings of his flock. The Lord looked with favor on Abel and his offering, ⁵but on Cain and his offering he did not look with favor. So Cain was very angry and dejected. ⁶Then the Lord said to Cain: Why are you angry? Why are you dejected? ⁷If you act rightly, you will be accepted; but if not, sin lies in wait at the door: its urge is for you, yet you can rule over it.

---

dominate others?" "Why do we wear clothes?" "Why is childbirth painful?" "Why is work difficult?" "Why do snakes crawl on the ground?" "Why do we die?" Finally, the divine words recall the second creation story, in which God fashioned the human being from the ground, and reminds Adam that he will return to the earth from which he came. Immediately after hearing this, the man names his wife Eve. Naming her is an act of domination, and at the same time the name he gives her acknowledges the mutuality between man and woman, announcing the beginning of motherhood and Eve's role as the first mother, illustrating the complexity of human relationships.

God punishes the couple, but does not abandon them. Immediately after announcing the punishment, God arranges for their needs by providing clothes for them. In covering their nakedness, God removes their shame. This act of compassion establishes a precedent for what follows repeatedly throughout the Old Testament: when humans violate the terms of the divine-human relationship God finds a way to restore the balance by providing for the needs of the people.

4:1-16 The first murder

The story of humanity continues with the births of Cain and Abel to Adam and Eve, as God promised after the first sin. The divine acceptance

⏴ ⁸Cain said to his brother Abel, "Let us go out in the field." When they were in the field, Cain attacked his brother Abel and killed him. ⁹Then the LORD asked Cain, Where is your brother Abel? He answered, "I do not know. Am I my ⏴ brother's keeper?" ¹⁰God then said: What have you done? Your brother's blood cries out to me from the ground! ¹¹Now you are banned from the ground that opened its mouth to receive your brother's blood from your hand. ¹²If you till the ground, it shall no longer give you its produce. You shall become a constant wanderer on the earth. ¹³Cain said to the LORD: "My punishment is too great to bear. ¹⁴Look, you have now banished me from the ground. I must avoid you and be a constant wanderer on the earth. Anyone may kill me at sight." ¹⁵Not so! the LORD said to him. If anyone kills Cain, Cain shall be avenged seven times. So the LORD put a mark on Cain, so that no one would kill him at sight. ¹⁶Cain then left the LORD's presence and settled in the land of Nod, east of Eden.

---

of Abel's sacrifice but not Cain's is troubling, as it appears to show that God plays favorites. We are not told how the brothers know whether their sacrifice is accepted, nor do we know why God rejects Cain's sacrifice. Perhaps the fact that Abel offers the first of his flock, while Cain offers the first of his crops, attests to the high regard for shepherds in the eleventh century, when the story was most likely put in writing. The main point of the story, though, is in Cain's reaction to the divine rejection of his offering. The Lord's speech to him suggests that rejecting Cain's offering does not in any way mean divine rejection of Cain himself. Cain's task is to do what is right, rather than give sin a chance to overtake him.

Cain's response is to kill his brother, violating the divine-human boundary by trying to exercise control over life and death. The divine question that follows in verse 9 reminds us of the question to Adam in 3:9, "Where are you?" Here the Lord asks Cain, "Where is your brother Abel?" highlighting the alienation that results from sin (4:9). The divine question holds Cain responsible for his brother Abel's welfare. Cain's contemptuous response illustrates his nonconcern for his brother and his disregard for the deity. The Lord's punishment of Cain is an example of *lex talionis*, the law of retaliation that specifies that the punishment must fit the crime in both kind and degree: it must relate to the wrong that has been done, and must equal and not exceed the amount of wrong that was done. Cain will no longer be able to subsist as a farmer because he has violated the very soil that he works. As with Adam and Eve, God punishes Cain, but does not abandon him, instead marking him for special protection.

Descendants of Cain and Seth. ¹⁷Cain had intercourse with his wife, and she conceived and bore Enoch. Cain also became the founder of a city, which he named after his son Enoch. ¹⁸To Enoch was born Irad, and Irad became the father of Mehujael; Mehujael became the father of Methusael, and Methusael became the father of Lamech. ¹⁹Lamech took two wives; the name of the first was Adah, and the name of the second Zillah. ²⁰Adah gave birth to Jabal, who became the ancestor of those who dwell in tents and keep livestock. ²¹His brother's name was Jubal, who became the ancestor of all who play the lyre and the reed pipe. ²²Zillah, on her part, gave birth to Tubalcain, the ancestor of all who forge instruments of bronze and iron. The sister of Tubalcain was Naamah. ²³Lamech said to his wives:

"Adah and Zillah, hear my voice;
    wives of Lamech, listen to my
        utterance:
I have killed a man for wounding
        me,
    a young man for bruising me.
²⁴If Cain is avenged seven times,
    then Lamech seventy-seven
        times."

²⁵Adam again had intercourse with his wife, and she gave birth to a son whom she called Seth. "God has granted me another offspring in place of Abel," she said, "because Cain killed him." ²⁶To Seth, in turn, a son was born, and he named him Enosh.

At that time people began to invoke the Lord by name.

5 Generations: Adam to Noah. ¹This is the record of the descendants of Adam. When God created human

4:17-24 Genealogical note

The genealogical note that follows in verses 17-24 shows that Cain has several generations of descendants who develop different professions important to civilization.

4:25–5:32 Adam's descendants

The narrative returns to Adam and Eve, reporting that they have additional children. The comment that people then begin to call on the Lord by name is puzzling because it seems to come too early: the Lord reveals the name Yʜᴡʜ to Moses at the burning bush (Exod 3:14), long after the time of the first humans. It might reflect the religious practices in the eleventh century, when the passage was most likely set down in written form. It also attests to the beginning of formal acts of worship, associating them with the descendants of Adam from earliest times.

A detailed genealogy records Adam's line to Noah's three sons: Shem, Ham, and Japheth. The narrative points out that the people are made with the same characteristics as the first humans: in God's image, male and female, and blessed. The list in chapter 5 includes many of the same names

beings, he made them in the likeness of God; ²he created them male and female. When they were created, he blessed them and named them humankind.

³Adam was one hundred and thirty years old when he begot a son in his likeness, after his image; and he named him Seth. ⁴Adam lived eight hundred years after he begot Seth, and he had other sons and daughters. ⁵The whole lifetime of Adam was nine hundred and thirty years; then he died.

⁶When Seth was one hundred and five years old, he begot Enosh. ⁷Seth lived eight hundred and seven years after he begot Enosh, and he had other sons and daughters. ⁸The whole lifetime of Seth was nine hundred and twelve years; then he died.

⁹When Enosh was ninety years old, he begot Kenan. ¹⁰Enosh lived eight hundred and fifteen years after he begot Kenan, and he had other sons and daughters. ¹¹The whole lifetime of Enosh was nine hundred and five years; then he died.

¹²When Kenan was seventy years old, he begot Mahalalel. ¹³Kenan lived eight hundred and forty years after he begot Mahalalel, and he had other sons and daughters. ¹⁴The whole lifetime of Kenan was nine hundred and ten years; then he died.

¹⁵When Mahalalel was sixty-five years old, he begot Jared. ¹⁶Mahalalel lived eight hundred and thirty years after he begot Jared, and he had other sons and daughters. ¹⁷The whole lifetime of Mahalalel was eight hundred and ninety-five years; then he died.

¹⁸When Jared was one hundred and sixty-two years old, he begot Enoch. ¹⁹Jared lived eight hundred years after he begot Enoch, and he had other sons and daughters. ²⁰The whole lifetime of Jared was nine hundred and sixty-two years; then he died.

²¹When Enoch was sixty-five years old, he begot Methuselah. ²²Enoch walked with God after he begot Methuselah for three hundred years, and he had other sons and daughters. ²³The

---

that we find in 4:17-24, but they are not identical. The lists represent different traditions, both of which were preserved when the stories were written down. The list in chapter 5 involves ten generations from Adam to Noah, a number that is parallel to the number of generations from Noah to Abraham in chapter 10. We cannot know the precise ages of these early people, partly because we do not know how they reckoned time and partly because the ages are unrealistic by modern calculations. Life expectancy today is the longest it has ever been, but does not approach the ages recorded here. The ages highlight the passage of a long time after the creation, during which humans thrived but also sinned. Verse 29 singles out Noah, identifying him as the one who will reverse the curse of the ground that began with Adam in 3:17-19 and continued with Cain in 4:10-12.

whole lifetime of Enoch was three hundred and sixty-five years. ²⁴Enoch walked with God, and he was no longer here, for God took him.

²⁵When Methuselah was one hundred and eighty-seven years old, he begot Lamech. ²⁶Methuselah lived seven hundred and eighty-two years after he begot Lamech, and he had other sons and daughters. ²⁷The whole lifetime of Methuselah was nine hundred and sixty-nine years; then he died.

²⁸When Lamech was one hundred and eighty-two years old, he begot a son ²⁹and named him Noah, saying, "This one shall bring us relief from our work and the toil of our hands, out of the very ground that the LORD has put under a curse." ³⁰Lamech lived five hundred and ninety-five years after he begot Noah, and he had other sons and daughters. ³¹The whole lifetime of Lamech was seven hundred and seventy-seven years; then he died.

³²When Noah was five hundred years old, he begot Shem, Ham, and Japheth.

6 **Origin of the Nephilim.** ¹When human beings began to grow numerous on the earth and daughters were born to them, ²the sons of God saw how beautiful the daughters of human beings were, and so they took for their wives whomever they pleased. ³Then the LORD said: My spirit shall not remain in human

6:1–9:17 The Flood

A brief incident about the Nephilim seems to draw on an ancient story no longer known to us. It recounts further actions that blur the distinction between humans and God, with the result that God regrets having created human beings. Ancient people thought the heart was the locus of thinking and decision making. The statement that God's heart is grieved announces God's realization that something is out of place among human beings, and the consequent decision to destroy all life, with the exception of Noah, who finds favor with God (see 5:29). This note introduces the story of the Flood and its aftermath, when creation is destroyed and then re-created.

The earth returns to its primeval chaos when the waters cover the earth, bursting forth from the boundaries to which they were assigned at the creation. And just as a divine wind swept over the waters in the beginning, so the same divine act returns the waters to their boundaries after the Flood. (In contrast, in the Epic of Gilgamesh the gods are terrified, once they see the destructive flood they have caused, and which they are powerless to control.) Once the people are back on dry land, Noah's sacrifice convinces God never to flood the earth again. God re-creates the people, providing for their needs in the same way as at the creation, with one exception: permission is granted to eat meat as long as the lifeblood has first been drained

NOAH

beings forever, because they are only flesh. Their days shall comprise one hundred and twenty years.

[4]The Nephilim appeared on earth in those days, as well as later, after the sons of God had intercourse with the daughters of human beings, who bore them sons. They were the heroes of old, the men of renown.

Warning of the Flood. [5]When the LORD saw how great the wickedness of human beings was on earth, and how every desire that their heart conceived was always nothing but evil, [6]the LORD regretted making human beings on the earth, and his heart was grieved.

[7]So the LORD said: I will wipe out from the earth the human beings I have created, and not only the human beings, but also the animals and the crawling things and the birds of the air, for I regret that I made them. [8]But Noah found favor with the LORD.

[9]These are the descendants of Noah. Noah was a righteous man and blameless in his generation; Noah walked with God. [10]Noah begot three sons: Shem, Ham, and Japheth.

[11]But the earth was corrupt in the view of God and full of lawlessness. [12]When God saw how corrupt the earth had become, since all mortals had corrupted their ways on earth, [13]God said to Noah: I see that the end of all mortals has come, for the earth is full of lawlessness because of them. So I am going to destroy them with the earth.

Preparation for the Flood. [14]Make yourself an ark of gopherwood, equip the ark with various compartments, and cover it inside and out with pitch. [15]This is how you shall build it: the length of the ark will be three hundred cubits, its width fifty cubits, and its height thirty cubits. [16]Make an opening for daylight and finish the ark a cubit above it. Put the ark's entrance on its side; you will make it with bottom, second and third decks. [17]I, on my part, am about to bring the flood waters on the earth, to destroy all creatures under the sky in which there is the breath of life; everything on earth shall perish. [18]I will establish my covenant with you. You shall go into the ark, you and your sons, your wife and your sons' wives with you. [19]Of all living creatures you shall bring two of every kind into the ark, one male and one female, to keep them alive along with you. [20]Of every kind of bird, of every kind of animal, and of every kind of thing that crawls on the ground, two of each will

---

out. The reason for this stipulation is that blood is the symbol of life, and therefore belongs only to God. The rainbow sign of covenant flashes back to the seventh day after the six days of creation, the day set aside for honoring the Creator. Now God makes the rainbow the solemn sign of the promise never to destroy the earth in this way again. Thus the Flood story ends with the reestablishment of the relationship between God and all creatures.

The repetition of the names of Noah's sons in 6:9-10 (see 5:32) is the first indication that the narrative includes different versions. These two versions

Noah, by P. Troschel, 1659

come to you, that you may keep them alive. ²¹Moreover, you are to provide yourself with all the food that is to be eaten, and store it away, that it may serve as provisions for you and for them. ²²Noah complied; he did just as God had commanded him.

⁷¹Then the LORD said to Noah: Go into the ark, you and all your household, for you alone in this generation have I found to be righteous before me. ²Of every clean animal, take with you seven pairs, a male and its mate; and of the unclean animals, one pair, a male and its mate; ³likewise, of every bird of the air, seven pairs, a male and a female, to keep their progeny alive over all the earth. ⁴For seven days from now I will bring rain down on the earth for forty days and forty nights, and so I will wipe out from the face of the earth every being that I have made. ⁵Noah complied, just as the LORD had commanded.

The Great Flood. ⁶Noah was six hundred years old when the flood came upon the earth. ⁷Together with his sons, his wife, and his sons' wives, Noah went into the ark because of the waters of the flood. ⁸Of the clean animals and the unclean, of the birds, and of everything that crawls on the ground, ⁹two by two,

male and female came to Noah into the ark, just as God had commanded him. ¹⁰When the seven days were over, the waters of the flood came upon the earth.

¹¹In the six hundredth year of Noah's life, in the second month, on the seventeenth day of the month: on that day

All the fountains of the great abyss
burst forth,
and the floodgates of the sky
were opened.

¹²For forty days and forty nights heavy rain poured down on the earth.

¹³On the very same day, Noah and his sons Shem, Ham, and Japheth, and Noah's wife, and the three wives of Noah's sons had entered the ark, ¹⁴together with every kind of wild animal, every kind of tame animal, every kind of crawling thing that crawls on the earth, and every kind of bird. ¹⁵Pairs of all creatures in which there was the breath of life came to Noah into the ark. ¹⁶Those that entered were male and female; of all creatures they came, as God had commanded Noah. Then the LORD shut him in.

¹⁷The flood continued upon the earth for forty days. As the waters increased, they lifted the ark, so that it rose above

---

are not separate accounts, as we have in the two creation stories; rather, the two are woven together throughout the story, giving different sets of details that express the two different points of view while telling a single story.

Other signs of two versions are that humanity is corrupt, and that the Creator decides to destroy it according to J in 6:5-7, and according to P in verses 11-13. God instructs Noah to build an ark in preparation for a devastating flood in verses 14-22. The details suggest the P strand of the story: specific measurements and precise instructions. This ark, or box,

the earth. ¹⁸The waters swelled and increased greatly on the earth, but the ark floated on the surface of the waters. ¹⁹Higher and higher on the earth the waters swelled, until all the highest mountains under the heavens were submerged. ²⁰The waters swelled fifteen cubits higher than the submerged mountains. ²¹All creatures that moved on earth perished: birds, tame animals, wild animals, and all that teemed on the earth, as well as all humankind. ²²Everything on dry land with the breath of life in its nostrils died. ²³The LORD wiped out every being on earth: human beings and animals, the crawling things and the birds of the air; all were wiped out from the earth. Only Noah and those with him in the ark were left.

²⁴And when the waters had swelled on the earth for one hundred and fifty days,

8 ¹God remembered Noah and all the animals, wild and tame, that were with him in the ark. So God made a wind sweep over the earth, and the waters began to subside. ²The fountains of the abyss and the floodgates of the sky were closed, and the downpour from the sky was held back. ³Gradually the waters receded from the earth. At the end of one hundred and fifty days, the waters had so diminished ⁴that, in the seventh month, on the seventeenth day of the month, the ark came to rest on the mountains of Ararat. ⁵The waters continued to diminish until the tenth month, and on the first day of the tenth month the tops of the mountains appeared.

⁶At the end of forty days Noah opened the hatch of the ark that he had made, ⁷and he released a raven. It flew back and forth until the waters dried off from the earth. ⁸Then he released a dove, to see if the waters had lessened on the earth. ⁹But the dove could find no place to perch, and it returned to him in the ark, for there was water over all the earth. Putting out his hand, he caught the dove and drew it back to him inside the ark. ¹⁰He waited yet seven days more and again released the dove from the ark. ¹¹In the evening the dove came back to him, and there in its bill was a plucked-off olive leaf! So Noah knew that the waters had diminished on the earth. ¹²He waited yet another seven days and then released the dove; but this time it did not come back.

¹³In the six hundred and first year, in the first month, on the first day of the month, the water began to dry up on the

---

will have no steering mechanism; God will be its pilot. The J strand does not include instructions for building, but gives instructions for entering it (7:1-3). The J instructions for entering the ark call for seven pairs of clean and one pair of unclean animals, all of which enter two by two (7:1-5, 8-9), while P reports that one pair of each enters the ark in 7:13-16a. The death of all other creatures appears in 7:21 (P version) and 7:22-23 in the J strand. The report of the end of the flood comes in 8:2b-3a (J) and 8:3b-5 (P). The J strand includes sending out birds to check the progress of the receding

29

earth. Noah then removed the covering of the ark and saw that the surface of the ground had dried. [14]In the second month, on the twenty-seventh day of the month, the earth was dry.

[15]Then God said to Noah: [16]Go out of the ark, together with your wife and your sons and your sons' wives. [17]Bring out with you every living thing that is with you—all creatures, be they birds or animals or crawling things that crawl on the earth—and let them abound on the earth, and be fertile and multiply on it. [18]So Noah came out, together with his sons and his wife and his sons' wives; [19]and all the animals, all the birds, and all the crawling creatures that crawl on the earth went out of the ark by families.

[20]Then Noah built an altar to the Lord, and choosing from every clean animal and every clean bird, he offered burnt offerings on the altar. [21]When the Lord smelled the sweet odor, the Lord said to himself: Never again will I curse the ground because of human beings, since the desires of the human heart are evil from youth; nor will I ever again strike down every living being, as I have done.

> [22]All the days of the earth,
> seedtime and harvest,
> cold and heat,
> Summer and winter,
> and day and night
> shall not cease.

Covenant with Noah. [1]God blessed Noah and his sons and said to them: Be fertile and multiply and fill the earth. [2]Fear and dread of you shall come upon all the animals of the earth and all the birds of the air, upon all the creatures that move about on the ground and all the fishes of the sea; into your power they are delivered. [3]Any living creature that moves about shall be yours to eat; I give them all to you as I did the green plants. [4]Only meat with its lifeblood still in it you shall not eat. [5]Indeed for your own lifeblood I will demand an accounting: from every animal I will demand it, and from a human being, each one for the blood of another, I will demand an accounting for human life.

> [6]Anyone who sheds the blood of a
> human being,
> by a human being shall that
> one's blood be shed;
> For in the image of God
> have human beings been made.

---

waters (8:6-12). Finally, the divine promise never again to destroy the earth by flood appears in 8:21b-22 (J) and 9:11-17 (P).

The P strand relates that God establishes a covenant, or solemn agreement, with Noah and all creatures, never again to destroy the earth by flood. The sign of the covenant will be the rainbow: whenever it appears, God will remember the solemn promise made to Noah. The narrative repeats the word "covenant" seven times, highlighting its solemn significance for God and all creation.

[7]Be fertile, then, and multiply; abound on earth and subdue it.

[8]God said to Noah and to his sons with him: [9]See, I am now establishing my covenant with you and your descendants after you [10]and with every living creature that was with you: the birds, the tame animals, and all the wild animals that were with you—all that came out of the ark. [11]I will establish my covenant with you, that never again shall all creatures be destroyed by the waters of a flood; there shall not be another flood to devastate the earth. [12]God said: This is the sign of the covenant that I am making between me and you and every living creature with you for all ages to come: [13]I set my bow in the clouds to serve as a sign of the covenant between me and the earth. [14]When I bring clouds over the earth, and the bow appears in the clouds, [15]I will remember my covenant between me and you and every living creature—every mortal being—so that the waters will never again become a flood to destroy every mortal being. [16]When the bow appears in the clouds, I will see it and remember the everlasting covenant between God and every living creature—every mortal being that is on earth. [17]God told Noah: This is the sign of the covenant I have established between me and every mortal being that is on earth.

Several narrative elements in the Flood story parallel the first Creation story, illustrating God's creation and re-creation of the world. The chart below shows the similarities between the two stories according to P.

Narrative elements	*Creation in 1:1–2:3*	*Re-creation in 7:11–9:17*
Wind over waters/earth	1:2	8:1
Watery chaos	1:1-2	7:11-12, 17-20
Separation of water and dry land	1:9-10	8:3b-5, 13a
Birds and animals brought forth	1:20-21	8:17-19
Blessing on animals: "Be fertile"	1:22	8:17
Humankind made "in the image of God"	1:26-27	9:6
Humans brought forth, blessed: "Be fertile"	1:27-28	9:1, 7
Humankind given dominion over animals	1:28	9:2
Provision of food for humankind	1:29-30	9:3
God saw . . . it was "very good/corrupt"	1:31	6:12
Covenant signs of Sabbath and rainbow	2:2-3	9:9-17

Noah and His Sons. ¹⁸The sons of Noah who came out of the ark were Shem, Ham and Japheth. Ham was the father of Canaan. ¹⁹These three were the sons of Noah, and from them the whole earth was populated.

²⁰Noah, a man of the soil, was the first to plant a vineyard. ²¹He drank some of the wine, became drunk, and lay naked inside his tent. ²²Ham, the father of Canaan, saw his father's nakedness, and he told his two brothers outside. ²³Shem and Japheth, however, took a robe, and holding it on their shoulders, they walked backward and covered their father's nakedness; since their faces were turned the other way, they did not see their father's nakedness. ²⁴When Noah woke up from his wine and learned what his youngest son had done to him, ²⁵he said:

"Cursed be Caanan!
    The lowest of slaves
        shall he be to his brothers."

²⁶He also said:

"Blessed be the LORD, the God of
    Shem!
Let Canaan be his slave.
²⁷May God expand Japheth,
    and may he dwell among the
        tents of Shem;
    and let Canaan be his slave."

²⁸Noah lived three hundred and fifty years after the flood. ²⁹The whole lifetime of Noah was nine hundred and fifty years; then he died.

10 **Table of the Nations.** ¹These are the descendants of Noah's sons, Shem, Ham and Japheth, to whom children were born after the flood.

²The descendants of Japheth: Gomer, Magog, Madai, Javan, Tubal, Meshech and Tiras. ³The descendants of Gomer: Ashkenaz, Diphath and Togarmah. ⁴The descendants of Javan: Elishah, Tarshish, the Kittim and the Rodanim. ⁵From these ▷ branched out the maritime nations.

These are the descendants of Japheth by their lands, each with its own language, according to their clans, by their nations.

9:18-28 Noah and his sons

A brief genealogical note introduces the vague and puzzling incident between Noah and his son Ham. The story most likely alludes to an ancient Near Eastern story no longer available to us. From an etiological point of view it introduces viniculture and its positive and negative consequences, and also explains the negative attitude of ancient Israel toward the Canaanites: while it was Ham who violated his father, the narrative condemns his son Canaan for Ham's act.

10:1-32 Table of nations

A genealogy of Noah's sons and their descendants illustrates the widespread populating of the earth after the Flood. The genealogy is primarily

⁶The descendants of Ham: Cush, Mizraim, Put and Canaan. ⁷The descendants of Cush: Seba, Havilah, Sabtah, Raamah and Sabteca. The descendants of Raamah: Sheba and Dedan.

⁸Cush became the father of Nimrod, who was the first to become a mighty warrior on earth. ⁹He was a mighty hunter in the eyes of the Lord; hence the saying, "Like Nimrod, a mighty hunter in the eyes of the Lord." ¹⁰His kingdom originated in Babylon, Erech and Accad, all of them in the land of Shinar. ¹¹From that land he went forth to Assyria, where he built Nineveh, Rehoboth-Ir and Calah, ¹²as well as Resen, between Nineveh and Calah, the latter being the principal city.

¹³Mizraim became the father of the Ludim, the Anamim, the Lehabim, the Naphtuhim, ¹⁴the Pathrusim, the Casluhim, and the Caphtorim from whom the Philistines came.

¹⁵Canaan became the father of Sidon, his firstborn, and of Heth; ¹⁶also of the Jebusites, the Amorites, the Girgashites, ¹⁷the Hivites, the Arkites, the Sinites, ¹⁸the Arvadites, the Zemarites, and the Hamathites. Afterward, the clans of the Canaanites spread out, ¹⁹so that the Canaanite borders extended from Sidon all the way to Gerar, near Gaza, and all the way to Sodom, Gomorrah, Admah and Zeboiim, near Lasha.

²⁰These are the descendants of Ham, according to their clans, according to their languages, by their lands, by their nations.

²¹To Shem also, Japheth's oldest brother and the ancestor of all the children of Eber, children were born. ²²The descendants of Shem: Elam, Asshur, Arpachshad, Lud and Aram. ²³The descendants of Aram: Uz, Hul, Gether and Mash.

²⁴Arpachshad became the father of Shelah, and Shelah became the father of Eber. ²⁵To Eber two sons were born: the name of the first was Peleg, for in his time the world was divided; and the name of his brother was Joktan.

²⁶Joktan became the father of Almodad, Sheleph, Hazarmaveth, Jerah, ²⁷Hadoram, Uzal, Diklah, ²⁸Obal, Abimael, Sheba, ²⁹Ophir, Havilah and Jobab. All these were descendants of Joktan. ³⁰Their settlements extended all the way from Mesha to Sephar, the eastern hill country.

³¹These are the descendants of Shem, according to their clans, according to their languages, by their lands, by their nations.

---

the work of P, with narrative parts in verses 8-19 and 24-30 ascribed to J. The list, typical of Genesis, does not differentiate between people and nations, but names seventy descendants of Noah through his three sons. Japheth's descendants settle in the area north and west of the Fertile Crescent; Ham's around the Red Sea, northeastern Africa, and Canaan; and Shem's in the Fertile Crescent and Arabian Peninsula. This list of ten generations from Noah to Abraham parallels the ten generations from Adam to Noah in

³²These are the clans of Noah's sons, according to their origins and by their nations. From these the nations of the earth branched out after the flood.

11 Tower of Babel. ¹The whole world had the same language and the same words. ²When they were migrating from the east, they came to a valley in the land of Shinar and settled there. ³They said to one another, "Come, let us mold bricks and harden them with fire." They used bricks for stone, and bitumen for mortar. ⁴Then they said, "Come, let us build ourselves a city and a tower with its top in the sky, and so make a name for ourselves; otherwise we shall be scattered all over the earth."

⁵The LORD came down to see the city and the tower that the people had built. ⁶Then the LORD said: If now, while they are one people and all have the same language, they have started to do this, nothing they presume to do will be out of their reach. ⁷Come, let us go down and there confuse their language, so that no one will understand the speech of another. ⁸So the LORD scattered them from there over all the earth, and they stopped building the city. ⁹That is why it was called Babel, because there the LORD confused the speech of all the world. From there the LORD scattered them over all the earth.

chapter 5. It does not prioritize any of the peoples, but names all of them as beneficiaries of the covenant God makes with Noah after the Flood.

11:1-9 The tower of Babel

The episode brings together three motifs: the development of technology, the dispersion of humanity throughout the world, and the confusion of languages. It specifies that all the people just named in the genealogy speak the same language, highlighting the unity of all humanity under God. In verses 1-4 we learn of a plan and its implementation by the humans, and in verses 5-8 we see the Lord's plan and its implementation. The people use their technical skills to try to construct a substantial, very tall building that will reach up into the sky, threatening to blur the boundary between the heavenly domain of God and the earthly dwelling of creatures. The Lord sees what the people are building, and realizes the potential threat to the divine-human boundary. Rather than risk a recurrence of chaos the Lord confuses their language and disperses the people all over the earth, thus populating the entire world and removing the danger that chaos will return. In an etiological note, the narrative specifies the name given to the place: Babel or Babylon. The words are similar to our modern term "babble," or incomprehensible talk, characterizing Babylon as a technologically advanced place where confusion thrives.

35

The building of the Tower of Babel. Manuscript illumination.

Descendants from Shem to Abraham. [10]These are the descendants of Shem. When Shem was one hundred years old, he begot Arpachshad, two years after the flood. [11]Shem lived five hundred years after he begot Arpachshad, and he had other sons and daughters. [12]When Arpachshad was thirty-five years old, he begot Shelah. [13]Arpachshad lived four hundred and three years after he begot Shelah, and he had other sons and daughters.

[14]When Shelah was thirty years old, he begot Eber. [15]Shelah lived four hundred and three years after he begot Eber, and he had other sons and daughters.

[16]When Eber was thirty-four years old, he begot Peleg. [17]Eber lived four hundred and thirty years after he begot Peleg, and he had other sons and daughters.

[18]When Peleg was thirty years old, he begot Reu. [19]Peleg lived two hundred and nine years after he begot Reu, and he had other sons and daughters.

[20]When Reu was thirty-two years old, he begot Serug. [21]Reu lived two hundred and seven years after he begot Serug, and he had other sons and daughters.

[22]When Serug was thirty years old, he begot Nahor. [23]Serug lived two hundred years after he begot Nahor, and he had other sons and daughters.

[24]When Nahor was twenty-nine years old, he begot Terah. [25]Nahor lived one hundred and nineteen years after he

11:10-28 Shem's descendants

The narrative returns to the genealogy of Shem from 10:22-31, repeating the names of his descendants and adding information about the ages of the different people. The names are the same through Shem's great-grandson Eber, who has two sons: Peleg and Joktan. The list in chapter 10 focuses on Joktan's descendants, while chapter 11 lists those of Peleg. Five generations after Peleg, Abram and his two brothers Nahor and Haran are born. This point marks a transition in the narrative, away from the universal history of the human race to the particular saga of a single family: that of Abram. The genealogies illustrate Abram's ancestral link to the early generations of humankind, and establish a geographical tie to his ancient home in Ur, near the confluence of the Tigris and Euphrates Rivers (2:14). The stage is now set for the ancestral story.

THE ANCESTRAL STORY
PART I: ABRAHAM AND SARAH

Genesis 11:29–25:18

With the end of chapter 11 the narrative begins to focus on the family of Terah and four generations of his descendants: Abraham and Sarah, Isaac

begot Terah, and he had other sons and daughters.

[26]When Terah was seventy years old, he begot Abram, Nahor and Haran.

II. The Story of the Ancestors of Israel

Terah. [27]These are the descendants of Terah. Terah begot Abram, Nahor, and Haran, and Haran begot Lot. [28]Haran died before Terah his father, in his native land, in Ur of the Chaldeans. [29]Abram and Nahor took wives; the name of Abram's wife was Sarai, and the name of Nahor's wife was Milcah, daughter of Haran, the father of Milcah and Iscah. [30]Sarai was barren; she had no child.

[31]Terah took his son Abram, his grandson Lot, son of Haran, and his daughter-in-law Sarai, the wife of his son Abram,

---

and Rebekah, Jacob and his two wives Leah and Rachel and their maids Bilhah and Zilpah, and finally Joseph. Chapters 12–36 recount the saga of the first three of these generations, and chapters 37–50 focus on Jacob's son Joseph. The stories, like those in Genesis 1–11, were passed along by oral storytellers over hundreds of years. They were gradually collected and arranged into the narrative we have today. The different episodes in the saga reflect the concerns of the tellers and compilers, who used the stories to address the issues of their day. In this section we will focus on Abraham and Sarah (11:29–25:18). Then we will consider Isaac and Rebekah (25:19–28:9); next, Jacob and his wives (28:10–36:43); and finally Joseph in 37:1–50:26.

Chapters 12–36, like Genesis 1–11, are organized around genealogical summaries that mark the generations. In what is called the Abraham cycle, or stories about Abraham, a genealogical statement about Terah appears in 11:27 and of Ishmael in 25:12; in the Jacob cycle we find a genealogical summary about Isaac in 25:19; and in the Joseph cycle, a genealogical focus on Jacob appears in 37:2. Throughout these cycles the themes of divine promises of land, descendants, a nation, and blessing form the nucleus of the ancestral stories. Chapters 12–36 are a series of sagas, that is, prose narratives based on oral traditions, with episodic plots around stereotyped themes or topics. The episodes narrate deeds or events from the past as they relate to the world of the narrator. The sagas in these chapters are family sagas, or sagas about the family's past. They incorporate ancient Near Eastern literary conventions such as type scenes and specific family-centered motifs, which we will discuss as we meet them in the sagas.

11:29–12:9 The call of Abram

The transitional comments at the end of chapter 11 set the stage for the Abraham cycle by giving biographical information about Abram and Sarai.

and brought them out of Ur of the Chaldeans, to go to the land of Canaan. But when they reached Haran, they settled there. [32]The lifetime of Terah was two hundred and five years; then Terah died in Haran.

12 Abram's Call and Migration.
[1]The LORD said to Abram: Go forth from your land, your relatives, and from your father's house to a land that I will show you. [2]I will make of you a great nation, and I will bless you; I will make your name great, so that you will be a blessing. [3]I will bless those who bless you and curse those who curse you. All the families of the earth will find blessing in you.

[4]Abram went as the LORD directed him, and Lot went with him. Abram was seventy-five years old when he left Haran. [5]Abram took his wife Sarai, his brother's son Lot, all the possessions that they had accumulated, and the persons they had acquired in Haran, and they set out for the land of Canaan. When they came to the land of Canaan, [6]Abram passed through the land as far as the sacred place at Shechem, by the oak of Moreh. The Canaanites were then in the land.

[7]The LORD appeared to Abram and said: To your descendants I will give this land. So Abram built an altar there to the LORD who had appeared to him. [8]From there he moved on to the hill country east of Bethel, pitching his tent with Bethel to the west and Ai to the east. He built an altar there to the LORD and in-

First, they link Abram with his ancestors. The narrative reports Sarai's childlessness twice, foreshadowing the importance of that detail in the narrative. The couple takes part in the family's migration from their ancient home in Ur to Canaan, but their travels are cut short when they settle in Haran, near the northernmost part of the Fertile Crescent. There Abram hears the divine commission to leave his family and go where the Lord shows him. In 12:2-3 the divine promise to Abraham includes a great nation and blessing; in fact, the word "bless" appears five times here. The Lord will bless Abram, and in turn he will be a blessing to all the communities on earth.

For a great nation two things are necessary: children and land. The first is a problem because, as the narrative mentions twice, Sarai is childless. In ancient times childlessness was thought to be the woman's problem; that information helps us appreciate the stories from within their cultural point of view, even though modern medicine has given us a broader understanding of the causes of infertility. We will pick up this motif of childlessness several times in the ancestral story.

The second necessity for a nation, land, is also problematic because Abram and his family are nomads; they have no land of their own. This second problematic motif also appears frequently in the Genesis stories.

voked the LORD by name. ⁹Then Abram journeyed on by stages to the Negeb.

Abram and Sarai in Egypt. ¹⁰There was famine in the land; so Abram went down to Egypt to sojourn there, since the famine in the land was severe. ¹¹When he was about to enter Egypt, he said to his wife Sarai: "I know that you are a beautiful woman. ¹²When the Egyptians see you, they will say, 'She is his wife'; then they will kill me, but let you live. ¹³Please say, therefore, that you are my

Verse 4 does not record any reaction to the divine command on Abram's part; it simply reports that Abram obeys the Lord's directive, taking his family and all his possessions to Canaan. Abram's nephew Lot, whose deceased father Haran was Abram's brother, travels with the family to Shechem. The account gives Abram's age: seventy-five; he is not a young man when they begin this journey.

Shechem was already an established worship center by the time Abram and his family arrived there; in verse 6 the narrative refers to a holy place near a certain tree. Abram responds to the divine promise of land by putting his own religious mark on the place: he builds an altar to the Lord. The promise of land is problematic because, as the narrative points out, the Canaanites were already living there. The dilemma of land use and ownership recurs throughout the book of Genesis and the rest of the Old Testament as well. Abram then built a second altar to the Lord near Bethel, south of Shechem, along their route southward toward the Negeb.

In the ancient Near East the building of altars marked sites as places of worship to honor a particular deity. The altars Abram builds identify the sites as places holy for the worship of Abram's God. The building of altars also marks the piece of land as sacred to the builders. Abram, in building an altar, makes an initial claim to the land. The book of Genesis takes for granted the existence of other gods worshiped by other peoples. In contrast, the book of Exodus describes in great detail the cosmic competition between the Lord and Pharaoh, whom the people believed was the personification of the sun god. That contest ends with the Lord's great victory over Pharaoh and the Egyptians, assuring the escaping Israelites that their newly identified Lord can care for them as he promised Moses.

12:10-20 Danger to Sarai

The family's survival depends on finding adequate sustenance in the face of famine, leading Abram and his family to travel southwest toward Egypt. This episode is told in the form of a type scene, that is, a story that

sister, so that I may fare well on your account and my life may be spared for your sake." [14]When Abram arrived in Egypt, the Egyptians saw that the woman was very beautiful. [15]When Pharaoh's officials saw her they praised her to Pharaoh, and the woman was taken into Pharaoh's house. [16]Abram fared well on her account, and he acquired sheep, oxen, male and female servants, male and female donkeys, and camels.

[17]But the LORD struck Pharaoh and his household with severe plagues because of Sarai, Abram's wife. [18]Then Pharaoh summoned Abram and said to him: "How could you do this to me! Why did you not tell me she was your wife? [19]Why did you say, 'She is my sister,' so that I took her for my wife? Now, here is your wife. Take her and leave!"

[20]Then Pharaoh gave his men orders concerning Abram, and they sent him

---

includes several standard plot elements. A couple prepares to enter foreign territory, and the husband fears for his life because his wife is beautiful and the hosts might try to kill him in order to marry his wife. He arranges with his wife that she will pose as his sister, rather than his wife. She does so; the hosts see her, find her attractive, and take her to their leader. Difficulties arise in the leader's house because of the wife-sister; the leader discovers the truth about the woman; and the couple departs. The scene occurs three times in Genesis; twice with Abram and Sarai and once with Isaac and Rebekah.

The incident that begins in 12:10 includes the above elements. Abram's words to Sarai on the outskirts of Egypt lay out the background information: she will pose as his sister. Sarai makes no reply to his request; we are left wondering whether she agrees or merely acquiesces. No genealogical information is given about Sarai when the family is first introduced in 11:27-30. We assume that she and Abram were related in some way before their marriage because the narrative implies that they both came from the city of Ur. Furthermore, the terms "sister" and "brother" had a broader range of meanings in the ancient world than today; Abram might simply have intended to acknowledge that he and Sarai were relatives.

When they enter Egypt events unfold exactly as Abram predicted, and the Egyptian officials take Sarai to the house of Pharaoh and heap gifts on Abram in return. But the Lord intervenes and brings suffering to Pharaoh's house on account of Abram's deceit. The story does not tell us how Pharaoh learns the cause of his sufferings; it reports only that once Pharaoh realizes what has happened, he orders Abram to leave with his wife and possessions. The type scene includes several noteworthy details. First,

away, with his wife and all that belonged to him.

13 Abram and Lot Part. ¹From Egypt Abram went up to the Negeb with his wife and all that belonged to him, and Lot went with him. ²Now Abram was very rich in livestock, silver, and gold. ³From the Negeb he traveled by stages toward Bethel, to the place between Bethel and Ai where his tent had formerly stood, ⁴the site where he had first built the altar; and there Abram invoked the LORD by name.

⁵Lot, who went with Abram, also had flocks and herds and tents, ⁶so that the land could not support them if they stayed together; their possessions were so great that they could not live together.

Abram seems to be looking out only for himself. He fears for his own life because his wife is beautiful, but does not seem to consider the possible consequences for Sarai, who he anticipates will be the cause of his own danger. A further concern is that Abram jeopardizes the Lord's promise of family because the arrangement threatens to destroy Abram and Sarai's marriage, thus eliminating the possibility that they will have the children God promised them.

The narrative specifies that the punishment to Pharaoh comes from the Lord, assuring that the Lord protects the promise to Abram in the midst of Abram's actions that threaten to negate it. This episode is the first of many that address threats to the divine promises of land and descendants. The threat sometimes comes through human action, either of Abram or one of his family members, or by someone outside his family. At other times the threat comes from nature and the people's ability to find enough food to eat. In every instance someone does something that jeopardizes the divine promise, and then the Lord takes steps to avert the danger and assure that the promise is carried forward. In this episode Abram himself risks cutting off the possibility of having the children God promised by pretending that he and Sarai are not married. The Lord intervenes when events take their normal course, and assures that the promise will move forward in spite of human interference.

13:1-18 Separation of Abram and Lot

Leaving Egypt, Abram and his family retrace their path back toward Bethel and Ai, where he built an altar on his earlier journey through that region. By this time both Abram and Lot have accumulated great wealth in the form of livestock, precious metals, and tents. As the number of animals increases, the need for grazing land to feed them begins to strain the

⁷There were quarrels between the herders of Abram's livestock and the herders of Lot's livestock. At this time the Canaanites and the Perizzites were living in the land.

⁸So Abram said to Lot: "Let there be no strife between you and me, or between your herders and my herders, for we are kindred. ⁹Is not the whole land available? Please separate from me. If you prefer the left, I will go to the right; if you prefer the right, I will go to the left." ¹⁰Lot looked about and saw how abundantly watered the whole Jordan Plain was as far as Zoar, like the LORD's own garden, or like Egypt. This was before the LORD had destroyed Sodom and Gomorrah. ¹¹Lot, therefore, chose for himself the whole Jordan Plain and set out eastward. Thus they separated from each other.

¹²Abram settled in the land of Canaan, while Lot settled among the cities of the Plain, pitching his tents near Sodom. ¹³Now the inhabitants of Sodom were wicked, great sinners against the LORD.

¹⁴After Lot had parted from him, the LORD said to Abram: Look about you, and from where you are, gaze to the north and south, east and west; ¹⁵all the land that you see I will give to you and your descendants forever. ¹⁶I will make your descendants like the dust of the earth; if anyone could count the dust of the earth, your descendants too might be counted. ¹⁷Get up and walk through the land, across its length and breadth, for I give it to you. ¹⁸Abram moved his tents and went on to settle near the oak of Mamre, which is at Hebron. There he built an altar to the LORD.

---

relationship between uncle and nephew. A further complication is that the Canaanites and Perizzites inhabit the land. Abram's solution to the problem is to offer Lot whatever part of the land he wishes, a very magnanimous offer by Abram who, as the older of the two, has the first right of selection. Lot chooses the more fertile area along the Jordan River banks. The narrative foreshadows troubles to come by noting that, even though the area is fertile, its inhabitants are wicked. Lot then moves his flocks to his selected area, and Abram stays in the central region of Canaan.

The episode illustrates Abram's willingness to provide for his nephew, even at significant cost to himself. In verses 14-15 God immediately rewards Abram's generosity by repeating the promise of land and descendants. This time the promises are more expansive than before: Abram is promised land as far as he can see, with descendants too numerous to count. The Lord invites Abram to move about in the land that will be given to him. Abram travels to Mamre, at Hebron, his first stop in the land of Canaan; he builds an altar to the Lord as is his custom.

14 **The Four Kings.** ¹When Amraphel king of Shinar, Arioch king of Ellasar, Chedorlaomer king of Elam, and Tidal king of Goiim ²made war on Bera king of Sodom, Birsha king of Gomorrah, Shinab king of Admah, Shemeber king of Zeboiim, and the king of Bela (that is, Zoar), ³all the latter kings joined forces in the Valley of Siddim (that is, the Salt Sea). ⁴For twelve years they had served Chedorlaomer, but in the thirteenth year they rebelled. ⁵In the fourteenth year Chedorlaomer and the kings allied with him came and defeated the Rephaim in Ashteroth-karnaim, the Zuzim in Ham, the Emim in Shaveh-kiriathaim, ⁶and the Horites in the hill country of Seir, as far as El-paran, close by the wilderness. ⁷They then turned back and came to En-mishpat (that is, Kadesh), and they

14:1-24 Abram and the kings

Lot's choice of territory quickly becomes complicated when four kings attack Sodom and four other cities. The episode itself is complex in several ways. The historical and geographical details cannot be verified. Furthermore, Abram is portrayed here in a different light from the surrounding chapters; there he was a patriarch and shepherd; here he is the commander of an army. His troops set out in pursuit of Lot's captors, traveling as far as Damascus, far to the north. This incident in the Genesis narrative is probably a later addition, inserted to address a question that was pertinent to the writer, but beyond the scope of this commentary. We will focus on another incident, namely, Abram's meeting with the two kings, the king of Sodom and Melchizedek of Salem, on his return from Damascus. Melchizedek welcomes Abram and Lot by performing a priestly ritual.

Several of the geographical locations have been identified; for example, Salem is the ancient name of the city of Jerusalem. The climactic scene in the chapter is Melchizedek's priestly ritual to welcome Abram back from his rescue mission. This scene sets the stage for David's reign and the years that followed it: Melchizedek is both king and priest. The narrative identifies him as king of Salem, and then describes a ritual that involves bread and wine and a blessing of Abram by Melchizedek. Melchizedek blesses Abram in the name of "God Most High," the chief deity among the Canaanite gods. The serving of bread and wine might be a simple act of hospitality, or might also represent a religious ritual to celebrate Abram's success. Its larger significance is thought to lie in its foreshadowing of three realities: the religious importance of Jerusalem, the combined royal and priestly offices of the king of the area, and the eventual loyalty of Abram's descendants to the Israelite king in Jerusalem. In a similar incident in 2 Samuel 6:13, David offers a sacrifice to the Lord during the ceremony of bringing the ark into

subdued the whole country of both the Amalekites and the Amorites who lived in Hazazon-tamar. [8]Thereupon the king of Sodom, the king of Gomorrah, the king of Admah, the king of Zeboiim, and the king of Bela (that is, Zoar) marched out, and in the Valley of Siddim they went into battle against them: [9]against Chedorlaomer king of Elam, Tidal king of Goiim, Amraphel king of Shinar, and Arioch king of Ellasar—four kings against five. [10]Now the Valley of Siddim was full of bitumen pits; and as the king of Sodom and the king of Gomorrah fled, they fell into these, while the rest fled to the mountains. [11]The victors seized all the possessions and food supplies of Sodom and Gomorrah and then went their way. [12]They took with them Abram's nephew Lot, who had been living in Sodom, as well as his possessions, and departed.

[13]A survivor came and brought the news to Abram the Hebrew, who was camping at the oak of Mamre the Amorite, a kinsman of Eshcol and Aner; these were allies of Abram. [14]When Abram heard that his kinsman had been captured, he mustered three hundred and eighteen of his retainers, born in his house, and went in pursuit as far as Dan. [15]He and his servants deployed against them at night, defeated them, and pursued them as far as Hobah, which is north of Damascus. [16]He recovered all the possessions. He also recovered his kinsman Lot and his possessions, along with the women and the other people.

[17]When Abram returned from his defeat of Chedorlaomer and the kings who were allied with him, the king of Sodom went out to greet him in the Valley of Shaveh (that is, the King's Valley).

[18]Melchizedek, king of Salem, brought out bread and wine. He was a priest of God Most High. [19]He blessed Abram with these words:

> "Blessed be Abram by God Most
>   High,
>   the creator of heaven and earth;
> [20]And blessed be God Most High,
>   who delivered your foes into
>   your hand."

Then Abram gave him a tenth of everything.

[21]The king of Sodom said to Abram, "Give me the captives; the goods you

---

Jerusalem (see also Ps 110:4). These foreshadowings of future situations suggest that the material is among the latest in the Genesis narrative. From the vantage point of the monarchy, the Priestly editor included details about the past that link the people's current reality with those long-ago days when Abram was new in the land, demonstrating that the Lord's protection of the people extended back into their earliest history. In a manner consistent with the early Christian custom of linking Christ to figures in the Old Testament, the author of Hebrews drew a resemblance between Melchizedek and Jesus Christ (Heb 7:1-4).

may keep." ²²But Abram replied to the king of Sodom: "I have sworn to the LORD, God Most High, the creator of heaven and earth, ²³that I would not take so much as a thread or a sandal strap from anything that is yours, so that you cannot say, 'I made Abram rich.' ²⁴Nothing for me except what my servants have consumed and the share that is due to the men who went with me—Aner, Eshcol and Mamre; let them take their share."

15 **The Covenant with Abram.** ¹Some time afterward, the word of the LORD came to Abram in a vision: Do not fear, Abram! I am your shield; I will make your reward very great.

²But Abram said, "Lord GOD, what can you give me, if I die childless and have only a servant of my household, Eliezer of Damascus?" ³Abram continued, "Look, you have given me no offspring, so a servant of my household will be my heir." ⁴Then the word of the

15:1-21 The promise to Abram

The narrative resumes with another divine promise that the Lord will protect Abram and give him a great reward. The first announcement, in verse 1, is vague compared to the earlier ones, but Abram's response articulates the profound problem foreshadowed above: the Lord promises offspring, but Abram's wife is barren. The conversation has a prophetic tone. The phrase "the word of the LORD came to . . ." appears frequently in the prophetic books, as does the context of a vision. The expression, "Do not fear" also occurs frequently in the prophetic books, when the Lord offers assurance to the prophet about a pressing problem, and the prophet in turn reassures the people. This prophetic language in the Lord's words to Abram speaks to the special relationship that Abram enjoys with the Lord. What is more, even though Abram still has no children, the divine speech foreshadows a change by which Abram will have many descendants.

The exchange resembles other biblical forms as well: verses 1-6 resemble a call narrative and verses 7-21 include elements of a covenant ritual. We will look at the narrative from these two points of view individually. First, a call consists of a theophany or appearance of God, a commission from God to perform a particular task, a question or objection on the part of the one receiving the call, and a reiteration of the call followed by a sign of confirmation. Here Abram has a vision (v. 1) in which the Lord makes a promise to him. Abram questions the promise on the grounds that he is childless (vv. 2-3). The Lord repeats the promise, expanding on it and adding the sign of the heavens: Abram's descendants will be as numerous as the stars in the sky (vv. 4-5). The text then asserts that Abram's faith in God is a righteous act; that is, Abram is in a right relationship with the Lord.

Lord came to him: No, that one will not be your heir; your own offspring will be your heir. ⁵He took him outside and said: Look up at the sky and count the stars, if you can. Just so, he added, will your descendants be. ⁶Abram put his faith in the Lord, who attributed it to him as an act of righteousness.

⁷He then said to him: I am the Lord who brought you from Ur of the Chaldeans to give you this land as a possession. ⁸"Lord God," he asked, "how will I know that I will possess it?" ⁹He answered him: Bring me a three-year-old heifer, a three-year-old female goat, a three-year-old ram, a turtledove, and a young pigeon. ¹⁰He brought him all these, split them in two, and placed each half opposite the other; but the birds he did not cut up. ¹¹Birds of prey swooped down on the carcasses, but Abram scared them away. ¹²As the sun was about to set, a deep sleep fell upon Abram, and a great, dark dread descended upon him.

In verse 7 the commission seems to begin all over again in the form of a covenant ritual. The passage includes a historical introduction, an enumeration of the terms of the covenant, a sign confirming it, a list of the blessings and curses to follow obedience or disobedience, and an arrangement for promulgating the covenant. Verses 7-21 include most of these elements. The historical introduction announces that the same Lord who first brought Abram out of Ur is now giving him the land. In 12:1, when the Lord first instructed Abram to begin his journey, he was already in Haran. Here the text extends divine guidance all the way back to the family's departure from Ur (11:31), suggesting that it was the Lord who prompted Terah to move his family to Canaan. Then, as in call narratives, Abram responds with a question. (See, for instance, Exod 3:11; Jer 1:6).

The divine response is a call for a covenant ritual. This ancient Near Eastern ceremony involved cutting prescribed animals in two; then the two covenant parties walked between the pieces, binding themselves to the terms of the covenant under penalty of a fate similar to that of the slaughtered animals. The precise significance of the swooping birds of prey is not known; it can be understood as a way of expressing Abram's willingness to abide by the terms of the agreement even when danger threatens. Likewise, the liminal light of sunset highlights the unknown dimension of Abram's agreement with the Lord.

In verse 13 the text interrupts its description of the covenant ceremony to reiterate and elaborate on the Lord's promise of land. In addition, it alludes to a period of slavery that anticipates the exodus. Finally, a sign in the form

[13]Then the LORD said to Abram: Know for certain that your descendants will reside as aliens in a land not their own, where they shall be enslaved and oppressed for four hundred years. [14]But I will bring judgment on the nation they must serve, and after this they will go out with great wealth. [15]You, however, will go to your ancestors in peace; you will be buried at a ripe old age. [16]In the fourth generation your descendants will return here, for the wickedness of the Amorites is not yet complete.

[17]When the sun had set and it was dark, there appeared a smoking fire pot and a flaming torch, which passed between those pieces. [18]On that day the LORD made a covenant with Abram, saying: To your descendants I give this land, from the Wadi of Egypt to the Great River, the Euphrates, [19]the land of the Kenites, the Kenizzites, the Kadmonites, [20]the Hittites, the Perizzites, the Rephaim, [21]the Amorites, the Canaanites, the Girgashites, and the Jebusites.

of fire witnesses and confirms the sacred agreement the Lord has made with Abram. This particular ceremony does not include a list of blessings and curses or an arrangement to promulgate the treaty, as Abram still does not have a family among whom to publicize it. The covenant ritual solemnizes the divine promise to Abram, and also sets the stage for the next episode in the couple's efforts to have children.

Here the type scene of the barren mother appears. This kind of story involves a childless woman who gives birth to a son as a result of divine intervention. She takes specific steps to assure that her son will be successful, and often the son becomes a leader at a time of transition or crisis. The barren mother type scene has three models: promise, competition, and request. According to the promise model, a divine messenger appears and promises a son. That promise is confirmed, even though the recipient does not believe it. The son is born and receives a name that bears some significance to his life and work.

The Bible includes this kind of promise in the stories of Sarai here in Genesis, and also in the story of Hannah in 1 Samuel 1–2. The promises of sons to Zechariah and Mary in Luke's Gospel follow this model as well (Luke 1–2). Here the initial promise is not specific, only that the Lord will give Abram a great reward. Abram's question responds to the earlier promises in 12:2-3 and 12:7 that refer to descendants. In the formal covenant section that follows (v. 13), the divine response confirms the initial promise of biological descendants to Abram. Later in the narrative the remaining elements of the promise model appear.

16 Birth of Ishmael.

Birth of Ishmael. [1]Abram's wife Sarai had borne him no children. Now she had an Egyptian maidservant named Hagar. [2]Sarai said to Abram: "The Lord has kept me from bearing children. Have intercourse with my maid; perhaps I will have sons through her." Abram obeyed Sarai. [3]Thus, after Abram had lived ten years in the land of Canaan, his wife Sarai took her maid, Hagar the Egyptian, and gave her to her husband Abram to be his wife. [4]He had intercourse with her, and she became pregnant. As soon as Hagar knew she was pregnant, her mistress lost stature in her eyes. [5]So Sarai said to Abram: "This outrage against me is your fault. I myself gave my maid to your embrace; but ever since she knew she was pregnant, I have lost stature in her eyes. May the Lord

16:1-16 The birth of Ishmael

The narrative returns to the dilemma of Abram and Sarai's childlessness in the story of the birth of Ishmael to Abram and Hagar, Sarai's maid. Sarai proposes, in keeping with ancient Near Eastern custom, that Abram father a child through Hagar. While we today find this a disconcerting arrangement, it illustrates the importance of children in the ancient world. Large families with many hands to do the work were a necessity for subsistence. In addition, it was a point of honor for a man to father a large family who would carry on his name.

This very human story depicts Sarai's frustration, embarrassment, and jealousy; Hagar's disdain for Sarai; and Abram's quiet lack of involvement in the controversy that ensues. In fact, Abram responds to Sarai just as he did to God: he heeds her request. When Sarai blames him for causing the problem, he responds to her accusation by returning Hagar to Sarai's care as the law provided for slaves who overstepped their boundaries. But Sarai's punishment exceeds Hagar's crime, and as a result of Sarai's mistreatment the maid runs away.

Hagar, like Abram and Sarai, receives divine promises when the Lord's messenger finds her, questions her, and sends her back to Sarai. She will have many descendants beginning with the son she carries in her womb. The messenger gives a name to the unborn child, and interprets the name for Hagar. The naming of a child had several layers of meaning in the ancient world. The significance of the one who gives the name foreshadows the importance of the child. In addition, the specific name foretells something about the character of the child, or about the life the child will live. Here the message promises divine care for Hagar and her son; it also hints that the tension between his mother and her mistress will continue in her son's

decide between you and me!" ⁶Abram told Sarai: "Your maid is in your power. Do to her what you regard as right." Sarai then mistreated her so much that Hagar ran away from her.

⁷The LORD's angel found her by a spring in the wilderness, the spring on the road to Shur, ⁸and he asked, "Hagar, maid of Sarai, where have you come from and where are you going?" She answered, "I am running away from my mistress, Sarai." ⁹But the LORD's angel told her: "Go back to your mistress and submit to her authority. ¹⁰I will make your descendants so numerous," added the LORD's angel, "that they will be too many to count." ¹¹Then the LORD's angel said to her:

"You are now pregnant and shall
bear a son;
you shall name him Ishmael,
For the LORD has heeded your
affliction.
¹²He shall be a wild ass of a man,
his hand against everyone,
and everyone's hand against
him;
Alongside all his kindred
shall he encamp."

¹³To the LORD who spoke to her she gave a name, saying, "You are God who sees me"; she meant, "Have I really seen

generation between him and other peoples. Hagar in turn gives a name to the Lord, expressing her own incredulity that she survives the experience of seeing the Lord. The incident takes place by a spring, and the account ends with the etiological note that the spring, now referred to as a well, is named to acknowledge Hagar's religious experience in that place. We can assume that the place was known among the people who told the story throughout the generations.

The incident is significant in several ways. First, it demonstrates the Lord's continuing care for all the people, including Hagar. It also teases the reader, suggesting a possible solution to the problem of Abram and Sarai's childlessness. That possibility seems all the more realistic in light of Abram's advancing age.

This episode introduces another model of the barren mother type scene: competition model. That model includes five elements: a wife is childless; her husband has another wife; the rival wife gives birth to a child, causing conflict; God intervenes to give a child to the childless wife; and finally, a significant name is given to the child. Here Sarai has no children; she gives her maid Hagar to Abram for the purpose of bearing him a child; Hagar bears a son, causing conflict between herself and Sarai; and the child receives the name Ishmael. At this point Sarai still does not bear a child; that element comes only after several more delays in the narrative.

God and remained alive after he saw me?" ¹⁴That is why the well is called Beer-lahai-roi. It is between Kadesh and Bered.

¹⁵Hagar bore Abram a son, and Abram named the son whom Hagar bore him Ishmael. ¹⁶Abram was eighty-six years old when Hagar bore him Ishmael.

17

Covenant of Circumcision. ¹When Abram was ninety-nine years old, the LORD appeared to Abram and said: I am God the Almighty. Walk in my presence and be blameless. ²Between you and me I will establish my covenant, and I will multiply you exceedingly.

³Abram fell face down and God said to him: ⁴For my part, here is my covenant with you: you are to become the father of a multitude of nations. ⁵No longer will you be called Abram; your name will be Abraham, for I am making you the father of a multitude of nations. ⁶I will make you exceedingly fertile; I will make nations of you; kings will stem from you. ⁷I will maintain my covenant between me and you and your descendants after you throughout the ages as an everlasting covenant, to be your God and the God of your descendants after you. ⁸I will give to you and to your descendants after you the land in which you are now residing as aliens, the whole land of Canaan, as a permanent possession; and I will be their God. ⁹God said to Abraham: For your part, you and your descendants after you must keep my covenant throughout the ages. ¹⁰This is the covenant between me and you and your descendants after you that you must keep: every male among you shall be circumcised. ¹¹Circumcise the flesh of your foreskin. That will be the sign of the covenant between me and you. ¹²Throughout the ages, every male among you, when he is eight days old, shall be circumcised, including houseborn slaves and those acquired with money from any foreigner who is not of

17:1-27 The covenant with Abraham

The chapter relates an additional development that, on a narrative level, postpones yet again the fulfillment of the promise of children to Abram and Sarai. This episode is P's version of the incident told by J in chapter 15. Thirteen years have passed since Ishmael's birth when the Lord appears again to Abram and begins with a formal introduction, and then changes Abram's name to Abraham to reflect his role as father of nations. The terms of the agreement ask something of both parties. God repeats the promise of descendants and land, and promises to be their God. The people are enjoined to keep the covenant, that is, to adhere to the terms of the divine-human relationship, and all the males are expected to be circumcised. The origins of this requirement, given in some detail, are puzzling to us, but were undoubtedly understood by ancient peoples. What we do know is that the people living in exile in Babylon during the sixth century B.C.

your descendants. [13]Yes, both the house-born slaves and those acquired with money must be circumcised. Thus my covenant will be in your flesh as an everlasting covenant. [14]If a male is uncircumcised, that is, if the flesh of his foreskin has not been cut away, such a one will be cut off from his people; he has broken my covenant.

[15]God further said to Abraham: As for Sarai your wife, do not call her Sarai; her name will be Sarah. [16]I will bless her, and I will give you a son by her. Her also will I bless; she will give rise to nations, and rulers of peoples will issue from her. [17]Abraham fell face down and laughed as he said to himself, "Can a child be born to a man who is a hundred years old? Can Sarah give birth at ninety?" [18]So Abraham said to God, "If only Ishmael could live in your favor!" [19]God replied: Even so, your wife Sarah is to bear you a son, and you shall call him Isaac. It is with him that I will maintain my covenant as an everlasting covenant and with his descendants after him. [20]Now as for Ishmael, I will heed you: I hereby bless him. I will make him fertile and will multiply him exceedingly. He will become the father of twelve chieftains, and I will make of him a great nation. [21]But my covenant I will maintain with Isaac, whom Sarah shall bear to you by this time next year. [22]When he had finished speaking with Abraham, God departed from him.

[23]Then Abraham took his son Ishmael and all his slaves, whether born in his house or acquired with his money—every male among the members of Abraham's household—and he circumcised the flesh of their foreskins on that same day, as God had told him to do. [24]Abraham was ninety-nine years old when the flesh of his foreskin was circumcised, [25]and his son Ishmael was thirteen years

---

looked upon circumcision as the sign of their identity as exiles from Judah, in contrast to the Babylonians, who did not practice it. In keeping with the theory that the Priestly writers and editors lived and worked in Babylon during the exile, it is quite possible that this became an important sign of identity at that time.

Sarai also receives a new name, Sarah, from God, confirming that she will be the mother of the promised son. Abraham's incredulity, amazement, and joy on hearing the promise cause his marvelously human reaction, which is all the more touching because heretofore his response was simply to do what he was asked. His laughter foreshadows the name of his promised son: Isaac, or "laughter." But he remains incredulous, and gives God an alternative proposal, to make Ishmael the favored one. This suggestion gives God the opportunity to clarify that Ishmael will receive the divine blessing and promise of a great nation; but the son of the covenant will be Isaac, whom Sarah will bear within the year.

old when the flesh of his foreskin was circumcised. ²⁶Thus, on that same day Abraham and his son Ishmael were circumcised; ²⁷and all the males of his household, including the slaves born in his house or acquired with his money from foreigners, were circumcised with him.

◄ **18** **Abraham's Visitors.** ¹The LORD appeared to Abraham by the oak of Mamre, as he sat in the entrance of his tent, while the day was growing hot. ²Looking up, he saw three men standing near him. When he saw them, he ran from the entrance of the tent to greet them; and bowing to the ground, ³he said: "Sir, if it please you, do not go on past your servant. ⁴Let some water be brought, that you may bathe your feet, and then rest under the tree. ⁵Now that

----

The divine announcement that the birth of the child will take place within a year moves the promise a step closer to fulfillment. Then the narrative reports that Abraham circumcises all the males in his family as the Lord commanded. This brief note illustrates yet again Abraham's unwavering obedience to God's commands. The vivid storytelling details characteristic of J are combined with P's solemn description of circumcision as the mark of the Lord's people.

The promise model of the barren mother type reappears in this episode. The Lord appears to Abraham (still Abram at the beginning of the episode), promising generations of descendants in verses 2-10. Then in verse 16 God explicitly announces that Sarah will be the child's mother. In response to Abraham's incredulous response God reiterates the promise and gives a name to the promised child. But several more events must intervene before the child is born.

18:1-16a The three visitors

Once again Abraham receives the divine promise of a child. The text juxtaposes the appearance of the Lord with the coming of three visitors in the heat of the day, creating several questions about the meaning of the text. Is the Lord one of the three visitors? Do all three guests represent the Lord? How is it that Abraham sees three people and bows down in respectful welcome; but when he speaks he seems to address only one person? As the text stands, it points out that God is revealed through humans, and through what is at first glance a visit from three travelers.

Many details suggest extremes: the heat of the desert afternoon, the three men who are related to the divine in some mysterious way, ninety-nine-year-old Abraham's energetic greeting, the feast he asks Sarah to prepare

you have come to your servant, let me bring you a little food, that you may refresh yourselves; and afterward you may go on your way." "Very well," they replied, "do as you have said."

⁶Abraham hurried into the tent to Sarah and said, "Quick, three measures of bran flour! Knead it and make bread." ⁷He ran to the herd, picked out a tender, choice calf, and gave it to a servant, who quickly prepared it. ⁸Then he got some curds and milk, as well as the calf that had been prepared, and set these before them, waiting on them under the tree while they ate.

⁹"Where is your wife Sarah?" they asked him. "There in the tent," he replied. ¹⁰One of them said, "I will return to you about this time next year, and Sarah will then have a son." Sarah was listening at the entrance of the tent, just behind him. ¹¹Now Abraham and Sarah were old, advanced in years, and Sarah had stopped having her menstrual periods. ¹²So Sarah laughed to herself and said, "Now that I am worn out and my

for the visitors. Then one of the guests asks a question that would seem impertinent in ancient Near Eastern society, "Where is your wife Sarah?" Women did not share the table with men, and the visitors were surely aware of that custom. The question seems inappropriately familiar until the visitor's next statement reveals the reason for his inquiry: when he returns in a year, Sarah will have a son. The Lord made the same promise in 17:21; this assertion by the visitor confirms both the promise and the date.

Now it is Sarah's turn to laugh. We learn that she has been listening to the conversation from her place out of sight, and she reacts as did Abraham: she laughs at the thought of bearing a child at her advanced age. Without realizing, she anticipates the name to be given to the boy. The follow-up question, "Why did Sarah laugh?" comes from the Lord, not from one of the three guests, and is directed to Abraham. But Sarah herself responds, denying that she laughed. Yet the visitor/the Lord hears the laugh: the narrative explains that it is a sign of her fear in response to the awesome announcement she has heard, and the amazing future it represents for her.

The entire incident bespeaks complexity—the human and divine realms are blurred, singular and plural forms intermingle, the normally reticent Abraham extends gracious hospitality, seemingly impossible promises are made, private responses become public—in keeping with the complicated reality the visitors announce: this elderly couple will soon be parents. As readers, we are tempted to join in the laughter with mixed emotions of relief, amazement, and puzzlement in the face of the seemingly insurmountable obstacle of the very advanced ages of husband and wife.

husband is old, am I still to have sexual pleasure?" [13]But the LORD said to Abraham: "Why did Sarah laugh and say, 'Will I really bear a child, old as I am?' [14]Is anything too marvelous for the LORD to do? At the appointed time, about this time next year, I will return to you, and Sarah will have a son." [15]Sarah lied, saying, "I did not laugh," because she was afraid. But he said, "Yes, you did."

Abraham Intercedes for Sodom.
[16]With Abraham walking with them to see them on their way, the men set out from there and looked down toward Sodom. [17]The LORD considered: Shall I hide from Abraham what I am about to do, [18]now that he is to become a great and mighty nation, and all the nations of the earth are to find blessing in him? [19]Indeed, I have singled him out that he may direct his children and his house-

hold in the future to keep the way of the LORD by doing what is right and just, so that the LORD may put into effect for Abraham the promises he made about him. [20]So the LORD said: The outcry against Sodom and Gomorrah is so great, and their sin so grave, [21]that I must go down to see whether or not their actions are as bad as the cry against them that comes to me. I mean to find out.

[22]As the men turned and walked on toward Sodom, Abraham remained standing before the LORD. [23]Then Abraham drew near and said: "Will you really sweep away the righteous with the wicked? [24]Suppose there were fifty righteous people in the city; would you really sweep away and not spare the place for the sake of the fifty righteous people within it? [25]Far be it from you to do such a thing, to kill the righteous

Here the promise model of the barren mother type scene highlights Sarah: it is she who cannot believe the messenger's word, and expresses her amazement in laughter. The messenger confirms the promise, not directly to Sarah but to Abraham: when he returns in a year, Sarah will have a child.

18:16b-33 Abraham intercedes for Sodom

The narrative returns to Sodom, where it left off in chapter 14. While Abraham accompanies his three guests on their journey, the Lord reflects on whether to let Abraham know about coming events. The incident is not simply about the destruction of Sodom; in larger terms it is about the developing relationship between the Lord and Abraham. The Lord has made him the father and teacher of many nations; therefore the Lord gives him information that will help him fulfill that responsibility. The Lord decides to investigate the rumors of sin in Sodom and Gomorrah.

Verse 22 takes us back to the puzzling identity of Abraham's three visitors. We learn that the men continue walking while the Lord stays behind with Abraham, who engages the Lord in conversation. He starts with the

with the wicked, so that the righteous and the wicked are treated alike! Far be it from you! Should not the judge of all the world do what is just?" ²⁶The Lord replied: If I find fifty righteous people in the city of Sodom, I will spare the whole place for their sake. ²⁷Abraham spoke up again: "See how I am presuming to speak to my Lord, though I am only dust and ashes! ²⁸What if there are five less than fifty righteous people? Will you destroy the whole city because of those five?" I will not destroy it, he answered, if I find forty-five there. ²⁹But Abraham persisted, saying, "What if only forty are found there?" He replied: I will refrain from doing it for the sake of the forty. ³⁰Then he said, "Do not let my Lord be angry if I go on. What if only thirty are found there?" He replied: I will refrain from doing it if I can find thirty there.

³¹Abraham went on, "Since I have thus presumed to speak to my Lord, what if there are no more than twenty?" I will not destroy it, he answered, for the sake of the twenty. ³²But he persisted: "Please, do not let my Lord be angry if I speak up this last time. What if ten are found there?" For the sake of the ten, he replied, I will not destroy it.

³³The Lord departed as soon as he had finished speaking with Abraham, and Abraham returned home.

19 **Destruction of Sodom and Gomorrah.** ¹The two angels reached Sodom in the evening, as Lot was sitting at the gate of Sodom. When Lot saw them, he got up to greet them; and bowing down with his face to the ground, ²he said, "Please, my lords, come aside into your servant's house for the night, and bathe your feet; you can get up early

assumption that the Lord will completely destroy the sinful city and questions the Lord about destroying innocent people. He persuades the Lord to think again about this plan that is out of character for the Deity. Abraham continues to press the question until the Lord agrees that ten innocent people are enough to warrant saving the city. Abraham has grown from silently obedient to passionately protective, an essential trait for the one destined to father many nations; he convinces the Lord to spare the city for the sake of the few righteous ones. This scene does not mention the possibility of repentance to forestall the destruction of the city, as we find in the prophetic books. (See, for instance, Jer 8:6; 9:4; Ezek 14:6; 18:30.)

19:1-29 Destruction of Sodom

Chapter 19 begins with the visit of the other two of Abraham's guests to Lot. The word "angels" is the English translation of the Hebrew word meaning "messengers," and designates anyone who delivers a word on behalf of another person. Here the two are called "angels," highlighting the ambiguous identity of the three visitors in chapter 18. Later in this chapter

to continue your journey." But they replied, "No, we will pass the night in the town square." ³He urged them so strongly, however, that they turned aside to his place and entered his house. He prepared a banquet for them, baking unleavened bread, and they dined.

⁴Before they went to bed, the townsmen of Sodom, both young and old—all the people to the last man—surrounded the house. ⁵They called to Lot and said to him, "Where are the men who came to your house tonight? Bring them out to us that we may have sexual relations with them." ⁶Lot went out to meet them at the entrance. When he had shut the door behind him, ⁷he said, "I beg you, my brothers, do not do this wicked thing! ⁸I have two daughters who have never had sexual relations with men. Let

me bring them out to you, and you may do to them as you please. But do not do anything to these men, for they have come under the shelter of my roof." ⁹They replied, "Stand back! This man," they said, "came here as a resident alien, and now he dares to give orders! We will treat you worse than them!" With that, they pressed hard against Lot, moving in closer to break down the door. ¹⁰But his guests put out their hands, pulled Lot inside with them, and closed the door; ¹¹they struck the men at the entrance of the house, small and great, with such a blinding light that they were utterly unable to find the doorway.

¹²Then the guests said to Lot: "Who else belongs to you here? Sons-in-law, your sons, your daughters, all who belong to you in the city—take them away

they announce on God's behalf, "We are about to destroy this place" (v. 13). Their visit begins with events that parallel the visit of the three men to Abraham: Lot receives the two visitors and bows to them in respectful welcome. He invites them to stay, and when they agree he prepares a meal for them.

At that point the similarities end: the meal Lot prepares is quite simple in contrast to the elaborate feast Abraham arranged for his guests. This detail does not begin to foreshadow the horror that is about to take place. Immediately the sinfulness of the Sodomites becomes apparent in their determination to violate the guests. While today we find Lot's offer to give his daughters to the men horrific, it speaks to the high priority given to hospitality among ancient Near Eastern nomads: a host protected his guests, regardless of the cost. This incident clarifies the sins of the city of Sodom alluded to in chapter 18: rampant lack of hospitality and sexual aberrations.

The quick action of the guests saves both Lot and his daughters from the horror that might have ensued. The NABRE translation of 19:11, "with such a blinding light that they were utterly unable to find the doorway" is

from this place! ¹³We are about to destroy this place, for the outcry reaching the LORD against those here is so great that the LORD has sent us to destroy it." ¹⁴So Lot went out and spoke to his sons-in-law, who had contracted marriage with his daughters. "Come on, leave this place," he told them; "the LORD is about to destroy the city." But his sons-in-law thought he was joking.

¹⁵As dawn was breaking, the angels urged Lot on, saying, "Come on! Take your wife with you and your two daughters who are here, or you will be swept away in the punishment of the city." ¹⁶When he hesitated, the men, because of the LORD's compassion for him, seized his hand and the hands of his wife and his two daughters and led them to safety outside the city. ¹⁷As soon as they had brought them outside, they said: "Flee for your life! Do not look back or stop anywhere on the Plain. Flee to the hills at once, or you will be swept away." ¹⁸"Oh, no, my lords!" Lot replied to them. ¹⁹"You have already shown favor to your servant, doing me the great kindness of saving my life. But I cannot flee to the hills, or the disaster will overtake and kill me. ²⁰Look, this town ahead is near enough to escape to. It is only a small place. Let me flee there—is it not a small place?—to save my life." ²¹"Well, then," he replied, "I grant you this favor too. I will not overthrow the town you have mentioned. ²²Hurry, escape there! I cannot do anything until you arrive there." That is why the town is called Zoar.

²³The sun had risen over the earth when Lot arrived in Zoar, ²⁴and the LORD

---

a bit ambiguous; the Hebrew text reads, "And they struck with blindness the men who were at the door of the house, both small and great, so that they were unable to find the door." The incident confirms the Lord's assessment of the wickedness of the place, and the visitors urge Lot to remove his family at once, before the city is destroyed for its sins.

After all that transpires with the two guests during the night, we expect Lot to depart immediately. Instead, the angels must cajole and negotiate with him throughout the night. First, the fiancés of Lot's two daughters refuse to take the warning seriously. Then at dawn the angels press him to take the other members, but Lot hesitates. The visitors remove them from the house and insist that they depart immediately and not look back or stop. Lot still resists, and begs to be allowed to go to a small town nearby. The response comes from one angel, implying, as in the story of Abraham's guests, that the angel is actually the Lord, who agrees to accommodate Lot's request.

After all these steps Lot's wife violates the command not to look back, and she becomes a pillar of salt (see also Wis 10:7). This detail is a bit of etiological folklore: at the southern end of the Dead Sea, the salt deposits

rained down sulfur upon Sodom and Gomorrah, fire from the LORD out of heaven. [25]He overthrew those cities and the whole Plain, together with the inhabitants of the cities and the produce of the soil. [26]But Lot's wife looked back, and she was turned into a pillar of salt.

[27]The next morning Abraham hurried to the place where he had stood before the LORD. [28]As he looked down toward Sodom and Gomorrah and the whole region of the Plain, he saw smoke over the land rising like the smoke from a kiln.

[29]When God destroyed the cities of the Plain, he remembered Abraham and sent Lot away from the upheaval that occurred when God overthrew the cities where Lot had been living.

Moabites and Ammonites. [30]Since Lot was afraid to stay in Zoar, he and his two daughters went up from Zoar and settled in the hill country, where he lived with his two daughters in a cave. [31]The firstborn said to the younger: "Our father is getting old, and there is not a man in the land to have intercourse with us as is the custom everywhere. [32]Come, let us ply our father with wine and then lie with him, that we may ensure posterity by our father." [33]So that night they plied their father with wine, and the

create bizarre shapes, some of which resemble human beings; tour guides point out which is their own favorite "Mrs. Lot." Here in the story the presence of a salt formation is explained as Lot's wife's punishment for her disobedience. In fact, the woman probably suffered the same end as all those who remained in Sodom: the sulphur and salt destroyed everything. (Salt is a symbol of death and destruction; see Judg 9:45.)

Verses 27-28 recount that Abraham witnesses the destructive scene. Again we learn nothing about the reaction of this very reticent man, but we do find out that it is for his sake that God spares Lot from the debacle.

19:30-38 Lot and his daughters

The action of Lot's daughters suggests they are living in very isolated circumstances after the destruction of Sodom. While the incident with their father would be offensive to modern sensibility, it shows the daughters' desperation and ingenuity in assuring offspring for their family. The incident also serves another purpose; that is, the two sons become the ancestors of the Ammonite and Moabite peoples. Both of these groups were neighbors of Israel; this brief account establishes the reason for the animosity between them and the Israelites. In addition, the episode highlights the importance of having children in ancient Near Eastern society. It also serves as a reminder that Sarah still has not given birth to the promised child, a concern that

firstborn went in and lay with her father; but he was not aware of her lying down or getting up. ³⁴The next day the firstborn said to the younger: "Last night I lay with my father. Let us ply him with wine again tonight, and then you go in and lie with him, that we may ensure posterity by our father." ³⁵So that night, too, they plied their father with wine, and then the younger one went in and lay with him; but he was not aware of her lying down or getting up.

³⁶Thus the two daughters of Lot became pregnant by their father. ³⁷The firstborn gave birth to a son whom she named Moab, saying, "From my father."

He is the ancestor of the Moabites of today. ³⁸The younger one, too, gave birth to a son, and she named him Ammon, saying, "The son of my kin." He is the ancestor of the Ammonites of today.

Abraham at Gerar. ¹From there Abraham journeyed on to the region of the Negeb, where he settled between Kadesh and Shur. While he resided in Gerar as an alien, ²Abraham said of his wife Sarah, "She is my sister." So Abimelech, king of Gerar, sent and took Sarah. ³But God came to Abimelech in a dream one night and said to him: You are about to die because of the woman you have taken, for she has a

becomes acute when the following incident threatens yet again to thwart the divine promise of a son.

20:1-18 Sarah endangered again

The story returns to Abraham and Sarah, repeating the plot of the wifesister story in chapter 12. This time the couple is in Gerar, and it is the local king Abimelech who takes Sarah into his house. This time Sarah explicitly supports Abraham's ruse by agreeing that she is his sister. God's warning to Abimelech saves him from punishment and saves Abraham and Sarah from further complications to their marriage. Abraham admits that fear has motivated him, and explains that Sarah is in fact the daughter of his father but not his mother; she is his half-sister. (We recall that the initial genealogy in Gen 11:27-29 does not include any mention of Sarah's lineage.) Once again we are reminded that Sarah still has no son, in contrast to the women of Gerar, whom God healed after their wombs had been closed in punishment for Abimelech's unwitting action. The event raises a question: Abraham puts the life of his wife in jeopardy because of his fear for his own life. How will he care for a newborn child, when he cares more for his own life than for his wife's?

It is problematic for us today to see the extent to which other people suffer the consequences of Abraham's efforts to protect himself. It is helpful

husband. ⁴Abimelech, who had not approached her, said: "O Lord, would you kill an innocent man? ⁵Was he not the one who told me, 'She is my sister'? She herself also stated, 'He is my brother.' I acted with pure heart and with clean hands." ⁶God answered him in the dream: Yes, I know you did it with a pure heart. In fact, it was I who kept you from sinning against me; that is why I did not let you touch her. ⁷So now, return the man's wife so that he may intercede for you, since he is a prophet, that you may live. If you do not return her, you can be sure that you and all who are yours will die.

⁸Early the next morning Abimelech called all his servants and informed them of everything that had happened, and the men were filled with fear. ⁹Then Abimelech summoned Abraham and said to him: "What have you done to us! What wrong did I do to you that you would have brought such great guilt on me and my kingdom? You have treated me in an intolerable way. ¹⁰What did you have in mind," Abimelech asked him, "that you would do such a thing?" ¹¹Abraham answered, "I thought there would be no fear of God in this place, and so they would kill me on account of my wife. ¹²Besides, she really is my sister, but only my father's daughter, not my mother's; and so she became my wife. ¹³When God sent me wandering from my father's house, I asked her: 'Would you do me this favor? In whatever place we come to, say: He is my brother.'"

¹⁴Then Abimelech took flocks and herds and male and female slaves and gave them to Abraham; and he restored his wife Sarah to him. ¹⁵Then Abimelech said, "Here, my land is at your disposal; settle wherever you please." ¹⁶To Sarah he said: "I hereby give your brother a thousand shekels of silver. This will pre-

---

to keep in mind that ancient people had a much stronger appreciation for the consequences of individual actions than we do today: they realized that every action affects all of creation. They understood that Abraham's actions to protect himself had ramifications for everyone: his family members, Abimelech, and all the people. In addition, we see an example of *lex talionis*, the law of retribution that insists that a punishment fit the crime. Here, the life of Sarah's promised child is endangered, and in consequence the future of Gerar is jeopardized.

But Abraham becomes the intercessor for the inhabitants of Gerar. Verse 17 reports that Abraham prays for Abimelech and his women, and as a result the Lord removes the punishment of sterility from them. Abraham's concern for a family other than his own represents a broadening awareness for the well-being of everyone. (We recall that Abraham urges God to spare the city of Sodom if a few righteous people can be found there; here Abraham convinces God to reverse the punishment he and Sarah caused by their ruse.)

serve your honor before all who are with you and will exonerate you before everyone." [17]Abraham then interceded with God, and God restored health to Abimelech, to his wife, and his maidservants, so that they bore children; [18]for the Lord had closed every womb in Abimelech's household on account of Abraham's wife Sarah.

21 **Birth of Isaac.** [1]The Lord took note of Sarah as he had said he would; the Lord did for her as he had promised. [2]Sarah became pregnant and bore Abraham a son in his old age, at the set time that God had stated. [3]Abraham gave the name Isaac to this son of his whom Sarah bore him. [4]When his son Isaac was eight days old, Abraham circumcised him, as God had commanded. [5]Abraham was a hundred years old when his son Isaac was born to him. [6]Sarah then said, "God has given me cause to laugh, and all who hear of it will laugh with me. [7]Who would ever have told Abraham," she added, "that Sarah would nurse children! Yet I have borne him a son in his old age." [8]The child grew and was weaned, and Abraham held a great banquet on the day of the child's weaning.

[9]Sarah noticed the son whom Hagar the Egyptian had borne to Abraham

21:1-21 Birth of Isaac and banishment of Hagar and Ishmael

At last the narrative reports that Sarah is pregnant and bears the promised son. He is circumcised and receives the promised name of Isaac. This time his name, "Laughter," relates to the joy his birth brings to his parents and all their acquaintances. The detail about Isaac's circumcision illustrates P's attention to details about religious practice: here we learn that Abraham carefully observes the covenant.

But in verse 9 the threats to the promise continue; Sarah works to ensure a future for her son in spite of her fear that Ishmael is a threat to him. Abraham's love for both his sons is evident in his distress over Sarah's demand (v. 11). The Lord reassures him that Ishmael, too, will receive divine protection and will himself become the ancestor of a great nation for Abraham's sake. This incident reminds us of Sarah's earlier insistence that Hagar leave, when the slave woman lorded it over Sarah because of Ishmael (ch. 16). This time it is Sarah's jealousy that prompts her to request that Hagar and Ishmael go away.

In verses 14-17 grief permeates the separation of Hagar and Ishmael from Abraham. The narrative describes in detail Abraham's preparations to send the two away, followed by Hagar and Ishmael's hopeless meandering and forlorn cries in the wilderness. The divine reassurance is more than words: God promises a future for Ishmael, then provides a well, insuring

playing with her son Isaac; [10]so she demanded of Abraham: "Drive out that slave and her son! No son of that slave is going to share the inheritance with my son Isaac!" [11]Abraham was greatly distressed because it concerned a son of his. [12]But God said to Abraham: Do not be distressed about the boy or about your slave woman. Obey Sarah, no matter what she asks of you; for it is through Isaac that descendants will bear your name. [13]As for the son of the slave woman, I will make a nation of him also, since he too is your offspring.

[14]Early the next morning Abraham got some bread and a skin of water and gave them to Hagar. Then, placing the child on her back, he sent her away. As she roamed aimlessly in the wilderness of Beer-sheba, [15]the water in the skin was used up. So she put the child down under one of the bushes, [16]and then went and sat down opposite him, about a bowshot away; for she said to herself, "I cannot watch the child die." As she sat opposite him, she wept aloud. [17]God heard the boy's voice, and God's angel called to Hagar from heaven: "What is the matter, Hagar? Do not fear; God has heard the boy's voice in this plight of his. [18]Get up, lift up the boy and hold him by the hand; for I will make of him a great nation." [19]Then God opened her eyes, and she saw a well of water. She went and filled the skin with water, and then let the boy drink.

[20]God was with the boy as he grew up. He lived in the wilderness and became an expert bowman. [21]He lived in the wilderness of Paran. His mother got a wife for him from the land of Egypt.

The Covenant at Beer-sheba. [22]At that time Abimelech, accompanied by Phicol, the commander of his army, said to Abraham: "God is with you in everything you do. [23]So now, swear to me by

they will have as much water as they need. (We will meet Ishmael's Egyptian descendants in chapter 37, when they rescue Joseph from the cistern, another place associated with water, where his brothers leave him.) Here the narrative anticipates the agonizing scene in chapter 22, when God asks Abraham to give up his son Isaac: both describe God's instructions to Abraham to give up his son, both enumerate Abraham's preparations in measured detail, both tell us the boy cries out, and in the end both tell of divine intervention on behalf of the boy.

Sarah's action to ensure her son's future completes the type scene of the barren mother. She does what she considers necessary in order to guarantee that Isaac will be the son who receives his father's inheritance.

21:22-34 The pact between Abraham and Abimelech

In a flashback to chapter 20, we learn that Abimelech and Abraham negotiate a settlement to assure that their families can live in peace with

God at this place that you will not deal falsely with me or with my progeny and posterity, but will act as loyally toward me and the land in which you reside as I have acted toward you." ²⁴Abraham replied, "I so swear."

²⁵Abraham, however, reproached Abimelech about a well that Abimelech's servants had seized by force. ²⁶"I have no idea who did that," Abimelech replied. "In fact, you never told me about it, nor did I ever hear of it until now."

²⁷Then Abraham took sheep and cattle and gave them to Abimelech and the two made a covenant. ²⁸Abraham also set apart seven ewe lambs of the flock, ²⁹and Abimelech asked him, "What is the purpose of these seven ewe lambs that you have set apart?" ³⁰Abraham answered, "The seven ewe lambs you shall accept from me that you may be

my witness that I dug this well." ³¹This is why the place is called Beer-sheba; the two of them took an oath there. ³²When they had thus made the covenant in Beer-sheba, Abimelech, along with Phicol, the commander of his army, left to return to the land of the Philistines.

³³Abraham planted a tamarisk at Beer-sheba, and there he invoked by name the LORD, God the Eternal. ³⁴Abraham resided in the land of the Philistines for a long time.

22 The Testing of Abraham. ¹Some ▶ time afterward, God put Abraham to the test and said to him: Abraham! "Here I am!" he replied. ²Then God said: Take your son Isaac, your only one, whom you love, and go to the land of Moriah. There offer him up as a burnt offering on one of the heights that I will point out to you. ³Early the next morning

---

one another, and that both groups will have access to water. Then Abraham plants a tree to stake his claim to the territory and mark it as a worship site, like the altars he built earlier.

22:1-19 God tests Abraham

Chapter 22 tells one of the most poignant stories in the Bible: God's test of Abraham. In Hebrew, Abraham's first response to God is *hinneni*, a word that has no exact English equivalent. It translates, "Here I am," and connotes attentiveness, readiness, willingness. The word appears again in verses 7 and 11. Abraham responds before he knows that God is about to make an unthinkable request. God describes Isaac in three phrases that intensify the dreadful irony of the divine instruction: "Take your son Isaac, your only one, whom you love."

After all the promises of a son, and all the times the promise was jeopardized before Isaac was finally born, now, before giving the command to Abraham, God highlights how precious Isaac is to Abraham by describing his uniqueness in three phrases of increasing intensity. Only then does

Abraham saddled his donkey, took with him two of his servants and his son Isaac, and after cutting the wood for the burnt offering, set out for the place of which God had told him.

⁴On the third day Abraham caught sight of the place from a distance. ⁵Abraham said to his servants: "Stay here with the donkey, while the boy and I go on over there. We will worship and then come back to you." ⁶So Abraham took the wood for the burnt offering and laid it on his son Isaac, while he himself carried the fire and the knife. As the two walked on together, ⁷Isaac spoke to his father Abraham. "Father!" he said. "Here I am," he replied. Isaac continued, "Here are the fire and the wood, but where is the sheep for the burnt offering?" ⁸"My son," Abraham answered, ▶ "God will provide the sheep for the burnt offering." Then the two walked on together.

⁹When they came to the place of which God had told him, Abraham built an altar there and arranged the wood on it. Next he bound his son Isaac, and put him on top of the wood on the altar. ¹⁰Then Abraham reached out and took the knife to slaughter his son. ¹¹But the ▶

God give the command to sacrifice Isaac in the land of Moriah, a place that cannot be located today. Second Chronicles 3:1 refers to Mount Moriah as the location of the Jerusalem temple, establishing a connection between the test of Abraham and the offering of sacrifices in the temple. Today the Muslim Dome of the Rock stands over the rock that tradition identifies as the place of Abraham's sacrifice.

The pace of the narrative resembles that of chapter 21: it gives measured details of Abraham's preparations, prolonging the suspense for both Abraham and Isaac, and also for the reader. We wonder how God can possibly ask this ultimate sacrifice of Abraham after all the years of promises that culminate in the gift of laughter that Isaac brings to his aged parents. The chapter continues the theme of jeopardy to the promise that permeates the entire Abraham narrative even after Isaac's birth, as we saw in chapter 21. But this time it is the Lord, who made the promise of children to Abraham and repeated it over and over again throughout many threats to its fulfillment, who seems to jeopardize the promise. In the previous chapter, Abraham hesitates to banish his son Ishmael, but God insists; now Abraham has only Isaac, and God directs him to sacrifice that one whom he loves. This is to be a burnt offering, or holocaust. The expression appears six times in this chapter, highlighting its importance. In the time of Abraham it was the father who offered the sacrifice; after the temple was built and worship was institutionalized, the requirements stipulated that the offering was to

angel of the LORD called to him from heaven, "Abraham, Abraham!" "Here I am," he answered. ¹²"Do not lay your hand on the boy," said the angel. "Do not do the least thing to him. For now I know that you fear God, since you did not withhold from me your son, your only one." ¹³Abraham looked up and saw a single ram caught by its horns in the thicket. So Abraham went and took the ram and offered it up as a burnt offering in place of his son. ¹⁴Abraham named that place Yahweh-yireh; hence

people today say, "On the mountain the LORD will provide."

¹⁵A second time the angel of the LORD called to Abraham from heaven ¹⁶and said: "I swear by my very self—oracle of the LORD—that because you acted as you did in not withholding from me your son, your only one, ¹⁷I will bless you and make your descendants as countless as the stars of the sky and the sands of the seashore; your descendants will take possession of the gates of their enemies, ¹⁸and in your descendants all

be an animal without blemish, and that the priest would burn the entire offering at the temple (see Lev 1:3-17).

These details about the divine command suggest that the episode became part of the narrative late in the monarchy, when political and military events were testing the faith of the entire people. The scope of the divine command grows in horror with each added detail; here we realize that Isaac is a fitting offering because he is unblemished. Abraham's silence after his initial "Here I am!" is typical of his quiet acceptance of divine instructions throughout his life. Here it is all the more poignant in light of the dreadful act he is asked to perform: no words can adequately respond to this divine command. Just as God heard the cry of Ishmael in 21:17, Abraham hears Isaac's cry in 22:7; he responds "Here I am" a second time. Isaac's question about the sacrificial animal indicates that he, too, expects a holocaust, but does not at all envision himself as the actual sacrificial victim. In 21:17 God hastens to reassure Hagar; here in 22:8 Abraham reassures Isaac that God will provide.

The narrative continues at its infinitely slow pace, recounting the details of preparing the sacrifice with Isaac on top of the firewood. The matter is almost too much to bear. Not until Abraham holds the knife above his son does the angel stop his hand from performing the sacrifice and announce that Abraham has passed the test. The expression "fear of God" connotes awe, reverence, and obedience. After Abraham completes the sacrifice by offering a ram, the messenger repeats the divine promise of offspring, this time relating it to Abraham's obedience to God. After that the scene ends

65

the nations of the earth will find blessing, because you obeyed my command."

[19]Abraham then returned to his servants, and they set out together for Beersheba, where Abraham lived.

Nahor's Descendants. [20]Some time afterward, the news came to Abraham: "Milcah too has borne sons to your brother Nahor: [21]Uz, his firstborn, his brother Buz, Kemuel the father of Aram, [22]Chesed, Hazo, Pildash, Jidlaph, and Bethuel." [23]Bethuel became the father of Rebekah. These eight Milcah bore to Nahor, Abraham's brother. [24]His concubine, whose name was Reumah, also bore children: Tebah, Gaham, Tahash, and Maacah.

23 Purchase of a Burial Plot. [1]The span of Sarah's life was one hundred and twenty-seven years. [2]She died

with the ambiguous note that they return home; even the narrator is too exhausted to specify who: only the servants? Isaac?

There is no mention of Sarah in this story. We can only wonder about her reaction to the entire affair. In his tapestry that hangs in the foyer of the Knesset, or Parliament, building in Jerusalem, Marc Chagall depicted Sarah present at the sacrifice. Her presence in the tapestry expresses her agonized love for the son who brought laughter to her, and also intensifies the pain in the event: what mother could bear to watch her child become a sacrificial lamb?

The narrative explains that this is a test of Abraham's faithfulness, and that he passes it with flying colors. But the portrayal of Abraham the father is problematic. In previous episodes, he pleads with God on behalf of others. He begs God not to destroy the city of Sodom if a few righteous people can be found there (18:22-32). He objects when Sarah wants Hagar and Ishmael banished (21:11). But here, when God asks him to kill his only son Isaac, the son who has been promised repeatedly, the son whom he loves, Abraham's only response is "hinneni."

A brief genealogical note follows, informing Abraham and the reader that Abraham's brother Nahor has twelve sons including one named Bethuel, the father of Rebekah. This information foreshadows future generations of Abraham's family: Isaac will eventually marry Rebekah, and Isaac's son Jacob will marry Rebekah's nieces and will father twelve sons and one daughter.

23:1-20 Sarah's death and burial

Now that Abraham has passed his final test he spends his remaining days settling his affairs: purchasing a burial plot for his wife Sarah, securing

in Kiriath-arba—now Hebron—in the land of Canaan, and Abraham proceeded to mourn and weep for her. ³Then he left the side of his deceased wife and addressed the Hittites: ⁴"Although I am a resident alien among you, sell me from your holdings a burial place, that I may bury my deceased wife." ⁵The Hittites answered Abraham: "Please, ⁶sir, listen to us! You are a mighty leader among us. Bury your dead in the choicest of our burial sites. None of us would deny you his burial ground for the burial of your dead." ⁷Abraham, however, proceeded to bow low before the people of the land, the Hittites, ⁸and said to them: "If you will allow me room for burial of my dead, listen to me! Intercede for me with Ephron, son of Zohar, ⁹so that he will sell me the cave of Machpelah that he owns; it is at the edge of his field. Let him sell it to me in your presence at its full price for a burial place."

¹⁰Now Ephron was sitting with the Hittites. So Ephron the Hittite replied to Abraham in the hearing of the Hittites, all who entered the gate of his city: ¹¹"Please, sir, listen to me! I give you both the field and the cave in it; in the presence of my people I give it to you. Bury

---

a wife for his son Isaac, and distributing his assets before his own death. Verses 1-2 provide the background information in the style of P, the probable source for the episode. In verses 3-18 Abraham negotiates the purchase of land for a burial site. The negotiations proceed in stages: first, as a sojourner in the land, he petitions the local people for a burial place. They respond favorably and respectfully, inviting him to select the piece of land he prefers (vv. 3-6). In verses 4-15 the expression "bury one's dead" appears seven times, always with a possessive word that expresses relationship, love, and respect and highlights the purpose of Abraham's request. In verses 7-11 he designates the cave he would like, and asks the council to make his request to the owner of the plot, according to the custom. The owner offers to give the cave and its surrounding field to Abraham.

We learn in verses 12-18 that Abraham prefers to buy the land, and weighs out the stipulated price. His request to purchase the property raises two difficulties: first, he is an alien and is normally not entitled to buy land (Lev 25:23); and second, landowners are very reluctant to give up their land (1 Kgs 21:3). These negotiations take place in the presence of witnesses because it is an oral, rather than written, agreement.

The process of acquiring land for burial resonated with the people during the exile in Babylon, when they were without land to call their own. The P editors incorporated that concern into the ancestral story in such a way that the episode fits both the ancestral narrative and the exilic loss of land.

your dead!" [12]But Abraham, after bowing low before the people of the land, [13]addressed Ephron in the hearing of these men: "If only you would please listen to me! I will pay you the price of the field. Accept it from me, that I may bury my dead there." [14]Ephron replied to Abraham, "Please, [15]sir, listen to me! A piece of land worth four hundred shekels of silver—what is that between you and me? Bury your dead!" [16]Abraham accepted Ephron's terms; he weighed out to him the silver that Ephron had stipulated in the hearing of the Hittites, four hundred shekels of silver at the current market value.

[17]Thus Ephron's field in Machpelah, facing Mamre, together with its cave and all the trees anywhere within its limits, was conveyed [18]to Abraham by purchase in the presence of the Hittites, all who entered the gate of Ephron's city. [19]After this, Abraham buried his wife Sarah in the cave of the field of Machpelah, facing Mamre—now Hebron—in the land of Canaan. [20]Thus the field with its cave was transferred from the Hittites to Abraham as a burial place.

24 **Isaac and Rebekah.** [1]Abraham was old, having seen many days, and the LORD had blessed him in every way. [2]Abraham said to the senior servant of his household, who had charge of all his possessions: "Put your hand under my thigh, [3]and I will make you swear by the LORD, the God of heaven and the God of earth, that you will not take a wife for my son from the daughters of the Canaanites among whom I live, [4]but that you will go to my own land and to

24:1-67 A wife for Isaac

One more task remains for Abraham in order to assure the continuation of the divine promise of progeny to him and Sarah: that is to find a wife for Isaac from among his own people. The text does not include Isaac in these arrangements; after the heart-stopping account of his near-death experience, there is no further record of interaction between father and son. The episode revolves around Abraham's servant, whom Abraham sends to his people in Haran. The importance of both family ties and land is highlighted in the servant's question as to whether to take Isaac back to that land if the chosen woman refuses to accompany the servant back to Canaan. Abraham's emphatic response assures the servant that the Lord will find him a wife. The servant's gesture in verse 9 (putting his hand under the thigh of his master) relates to an ancient custom of swearing by the genitals in acknowledgment of their sacred importance for passing life along to the next generation. (The thigh is a euphemism for genitals.) A further consideration is the need for Isaac to remain in Canaan because he embodies the divine promises of descendants and land. Later the Lord instructs him not to leave the land, even in time of famine (Gen 26:2).

my relatives to get a wife for my son Isaac." [5]The servant asked him: "What if the woman is unwilling to follow me to this land? Should I then take your son back to the land from which you came?" [6]Abraham told him, "Never take my son back there for any reason! [7]The LORD, the God of heaven, who took me from my father's house and the land of my relatives, and who confirmed by oath the promise he made to me, 'I will give this land to your descendants'—he will send his angel before you, and you will get a wife for my son there. [8]If the woman is unwilling to follow you, you will be released from this oath to me. But never take my son back there!" [9]So the servant put his hand under the thigh of his

---

Abraham's wealth and his eagerness to make a good impression on his relatives are evident in the sizeable gift the servant takes with him as a bride-price. The journey is surely lengthy, given the distance involved and the number of cattle in the servant's care; but the narrative skips over any mention of the trip, and focuses immediately on the scene at the well.

This story is an example of another kind of type scene: the betrothal. The type involves a man traveling to foreign territory to find a wife for himself or someone else. Once there he goes to a well and meets young women of the area. Someone provides water from the well for the visitor and for the animals gathered there. Then the girls return home to announce the visitor's presence. He receives an invitation to their home, and a betrothal follows. This scene appears here and also in Genesis 29, when Jacob is looking for a wife. The type scene appears again in abbreviated form in Exodus 2:15-22, when Moses takes a wife after fleeing from Egypt.

Here, in accordance with the type scene, the servant goes to the well at the time when the women come to get water for the evening meal. The servant prays to God, then sets up the scenario by which he will know whom to request as a wife for his master. It is a simple device: he will ask for a drink of water, and if a young woman agrees to give water not only to him but also to his camels, he will know she is the one he seeks. The narrator tells the reader that Rebekah is the granddaughter of Abraham's brother Nahor, and thus Abraham's grandniece, but the servant does not yet know this.

The particulars give the story its unique character. The text describes Rebekah in an unusual amount of detail. Specifically, we learn that she is a very beautiful virgin, an ideal choice for a wife for Isaac. The type scene continues when the servant poses his question and Rebekah responds, giving him water and then making several trips back and forth to water the

master Abraham and swore to him concerning this matter.

¹⁰The servant then took ten of his master's camels, and bearing all kinds of gifts from his master, he made his way to the city of Nahor in Aram Naharaim. ¹¹Near evening, at the time when women go out to draw water, he made the camels kneel by the well outside the city. ¹²Then he said: "Lᴏʀᴅ, God of my master Abraham, let it turn out favorably for me today and thus deal graciously with my master Abraham. ¹³While I stand here at the spring and the daughters of the townspeople are coming out to draw water, ¹⁴if I say to a young woman, 'Please lower your jug, that I may drink,' and she answers, 'Drink, and I will water your camels, too,' then she is the one whom you have decided upon for your servant Isaac. In this way I will know that you have dealt graciously with my master."

¹⁵He had scarcely finished speaking when Rebekah—who was born to Bethuel, son of Milcah, the wife of Abraham's brother Nahor—came out with a jug on her shoulder. ¹⁶The young woman was very beautiful, a virgin, untouched by man. She went down to the spring and filled her jug. As she came up, ¹⁷the servant ran toward her and said, "Please give me a sip of water from your jug." ¹⁸"Drink, sir," she replied, and quickly lowering the jug into her hand, she gave him a drink. ¹⁹When she had finished giving him a drink, she said, "I will draw water for your camels, too, until they have finished drinking." ²⁰With that, she quickly emptied her jug into the drinking trough and ran back to the well to draw more water, until she had drawn enough for all the camels. ²¹The man watched her the whole time, silently waiting to learn whether or not the Lᴏʀᴅ had made his journey successful. ²²When the camels had finished drinking, the man took out a gold nose-ring weighing half a shekel, and two gold bracelets weighing ten shekels for her wrists. ²³Then he asked her: "Whose daughter are you? Tell me, please. And is there a place in your father's house for us to spend the night?" ²⁴She answered: "I am the daughter of Bethuel the son of Milcah, whom she bore to Nahor. ²⁵We have plenty of straw and fodder," she added, "and also a place to spend the

---

ten camels as well. These details depict Rebekah as energetic, industrious, and generous, further augmenting her desirability as a wife for Isaac. The servant's two questions remind us that he still does not know who she is until she unwittingly identifies herself as a member of Abraham's family. The type scene continues as the girl rushes home to announce the servant's coming while the servant prays in thanksgiving to God for leading him there.

In keeping with nomadic hospitality, Rebekah's brother Laban rushes out to the servant and invites him to his home. The servant insists on tell-

night." ²⁶The man then knelt and bowed down to the LORD, ²⁷saying: "Blessed be the LORD, the God of my master Abraham, who has not let his kindness and fidelity toward my master fail. As for me, the LORD has led me straight to the house of my master's brother."

²⁸Then the young woman ran off and told her mother's household what had happened. ²⁹Now Rebekah had a brother named Laban. Laban rushed outside to the man at the spring. ³⁰When he saw the nose-ring and the bracelets on his sister's arms and when he heard Rebekah repeating what the man had said to her, he went to him while he was standing by the camels at the spring. ³¹He said: "Come, blessed of the LORD! Why are you standing outside when I have made the house ready, as well as a place for the camels?" ³²The man then went inside; and while the camels were being unloaded and provided with straw and fodder, water was brought to bathe his feet and the feet of the men who were with him. ³³But when food was set before him, he said, "I will not eat until I

have told my story." "Go ahead," they replied.

³⁴"I am Abraham's servant," he began. ³⁵"The LORD has blessed my master so abundantly that he has become wealthy; he has given him flocks and herds, silver and gold, male and female slaves, and camels and donkeys. ³⁶My master's wife Sarah bore a son to my master in her old age, and he has given him everything he owns. ³⁷My master put me under oath, saying: 'You shall not take a wife for my son from the daughters of the Canaanites in whose land I live; ³⁸instead, you must go to my father's house, to my own family, to get a wife for my son.' ³⁹When I asked my master, 'What if the woman will not follow me?' ⁴⁰he replied: 'The LORD, in whose presence I have always walked, will send his angel with you and make your journey successful, and so you will get a wife for my son from my own family and my father's house. ⁴¹Then you will be freed from my curse. If you go to my family and they refuse you, then, too, you will be free from my curse.'

ing his story, explaining why he has come and reminding the reader that the Lord is guiding the events that take place. The family members readily agree to the servant's request that Rebekah return with him to become Isaac's wife because they recognize that the request is from the Lord. Their statement, "Here is Rebekah, right in front of you; take her and go" in verse 51 is the formal ratification of the betrothal. The Hebrew formula includes the word *hinneh* that we met in chapter 22 and that connotes attentiveness, readiness, and willingness.

The next morning, in verse 54, her family suggests that the party stay awhile before leaving, in keeping with customs of hospitality. But the

42"When I came to the spring today, I said: 'LORD, God of my master Abraham, please make successful the journey I am on. 43While I stand here at the spring, if I say to a young woman who comes out to draw water, 'Please give me a little water from your jug,' 44and she answers, 'Drink, and I will draw water for your camels, too—then she is the woman whom the LORD has decided upon for my master's son.'

45"I had scarcely finished saying this to myself when Rebekah came out with a jug on her shoulder. After she went down to the spring and drew water, I said to her, 'Please let me have a drink.' 46She quickly lowered the jug she was carrying and said, 'Drink, and I will water your camels, too.' So I drank, and she watered the camels also. 47When I asked her, 'Whose daughter are you?' she answered, 'The daughter of Bethuel, son of Nahor, borne to Nahor by Milcah.' So I put the ring on her nose and the bracelets on her wrists. 48Then I knelt and bowed down to the LORD, blessing the LORD, the God of my master Abraham, who had led me on the right road to obtain the daughter of my master's kinsman for his son. 49Now, if you will act with kindness and fidelity toward my master, let me know; but if not, let me know that too. I can then proceed accordingly."

50Laban and Bethuel said in reply: "This thing comes from the LORD; we can say nothing to you either for or against it. 51Here is Rebekah, right in front of you; take her and go, that she may become the wife of your master's son, as the LORD has said." 52When Abraham's servant heard their answer, he bowed to the ground before the LORD. 53Then he brought out objects of silver and gold and clothing and presented them to Rebekah; he also gave costly presents to her brother and mother. 54After he and the men with him had eaten and drunk, they spent the night there.

---

servant is eager to return to Abraham and report the successful outcome of his trip. The family members ask Rebekah's consent to the arrangement. This is a necessary step in ancient Near Eastern societies, because the betrothal involves two special circumstances: the marriage is arranged by her brother rather than her father, and it will take her away from her homeland. As soon as she gives her consent the family members send her and her nurse with the servant and all his retinue. The fact that her nurse accompanies her suggests that Rebekah is still quite young at the time of the betrothal. Her family members bless her with the hope of many descendants as well as victory over enemies. (See Ruth 4:11 for a similar blessing.)

In verse 62 Isaac reappears in the story for the first time since his near-sacrifice. We learn that he is living in the Negeb, and that one day in the late afternoon he sees the approaching caravan. The Hebrew text is not clear here, so we do not know whether he has been expecting them. The narra-

When they got up the next morning, he said, "Allow me to return to my master." ⁵⁵Her brother and mother replied, "Let the young woman stay with us a short while, say ten days; after that she may go." ⁵⁶But he said to them, "Do not detain me, now that the Lord has made my journey successful; let me go back to my master." ⁵⁷They answered, "Let us call the young woman and see what she herself has to say about it." ⁵⁸So they called Rebekah and asked her, "Will you go with this man?" She answered, "I will." ⁵⁹At this they sent off their sister Rebekah and her nurse with Abraham's servant and his men. ⁶⁰They blessed Rebekah and said:

"Sister, may you grow
  into thousands of myriads;
And may your descendants gain
    possession
  of the gates of their enemies!"

⁶¹Then Rebekah and her attendants started out; they mounted the camels and followed the man. So the servant took Rebekah and went on his way.

⁶²Meanwhile Isaac had gone from Beer-lahai-roi and was living in the region of the Negeb. ⁶³One day toward evening he went out to walk in the field, and caught sight of camels approaching. ⁶⁴Rebekah, too, caught sight of Isaac, and got down from her camel. ⁶⁵She asked the servant, "Who is the man over there, walking through the fields toward us?" "That is my master," replied the servant. Then she took her veil and covered herself.

⁶⁶The servant recounted to Isaac all the things he had done. ⁶⁷Then Isaac brought Rebekah into the tent of his mother Sarah. He took Rebekah as his wife. Isaac loved her and found solace after the death of his mother.

---

tive switches immediately to Rebekah, who looks up at the same time and sees Isaac. The simple description of their meeting is anticlimactic after the lengthy account of the servant's journey to find Rebekah and bring her home with him. Rebekah veils herself for their meeting, signaling to Isaac that she has come to marry him.

The servant's response, "That is my master," is puzzling here, as his master is actually Abraham, but the person in front of them is Isaac. It is possible that Abraham has died by the time the party returns. That would explain the servant's comment in verse 36 that Abraham has given everything he owns to his son Isaac, and also the note that the servant reports on his journey to Isaac (v. 66). Abraham's death is actually announced in chapter 25, immediately after the finding of a wife for Isaac, perhaps so as not to interrupt the flow of events in chapter 24. The touching note that Rebekah is a comfort to Isaac after his mother Sarah's death suggests that Isaac misses her keenly.

25

Abraham's Sons by Keturah. [1]Abraham took another wife, whose name was Keturah. [2]She bore him Zimran, Jokshan, Medan, Midian, Ishbak, and Shuah. [3]Jokshan became the father of Sheba and Dedan. The descendants of Dedan were the Asshurim, the Letushim, and the Leummim. [4]The descendants of Midian were Ephah, Epher, Hanoch, Abida, and Eldaah. All of these were descendants of Keturah.

[5]Abraham gave everything that he owned to his son Isaac. [6]To the sons of his concubines, however, he gave gifts while he was still living, as he sent them away eastward, to the land of Kedem, away from his son Isaac.

Death of Abraham. [7]The whole span of Abraham's life was one hundred and seventy-five years. [8]Then he breathed his last, dying at a ripe old age, grown old after a full life; and he was gathered to his people. [9]His sons Isaac and Ishmael buried him in the cave of Machpelah, in the field of Ephron, son of Zohar the Hittite, which faces Mamre, [10]the field that Abraham had bought from the Hittites; there he was buried next to his wife Sarah. [11]After the death of Abraham, God blessed his son Isaac, who lived near Beer-lahai-roi.

Descendants of Ishmael. [12]These are the descendants of Abraham's son Ishmael, whom Hagar the Egyptian, Sarah's slave, bore to Abraham. [13]These are the names of Ishmael's sons, listed in the order of their birth: Ishmael's firstborn Nebaioth, Kedar, Adbeel, Mibsam, [14]Mishma, Dumah, Massa, [15]Hadad, Tema, Jetur, Naphish, and Kedemah. [16]These are the sons of Ishmael, their names by their villages and encamp-

---

25:1-18 Abraham's death and burial

Chapter 25 begins with a genealogical summary of Abraham's descendants through his second wife Keturah. It specifies that Isaac receives his entire inheritance (see 24:36); but Abraham made settlements with his other sons, and sent them away to the east. This arrangement honors his relationship with all his sons, and at the same time protects the divine promises and the special status of his son Isaac who will carry the promise into the next generation.

Abraham dies, having left all his affairs in order. His sons Isaac and Ishmael bury him next to his wife Sarah. Another genealogical note lists the twelve sons of Ishmael, who become tribal chieftains. The narrative then records Ishmael's death, and gives the extent of the territory in which his descendants live in fulfillment of the promise in 21:13. This section brings to a conclusion the account of Abraham's and Ishmael's lives. It now picks up the thread of Isaac's life at the point of his marriage to Rebekah and the beginning of a new generation who will carry forward the divine promises of descendants and land.

ments; twelve chieftains of as many tribal groups.

[17]The span of Ishmael's life was one hundred and thirty-seven years. After he had breathed his last and died, he was gathered to his people. [18]The Ishmaelites ranged from Havilah, by Shur, which is on the border of Egypt, all the way to Asshur; and they pitched camp alongside their various kindred.

Birth of Esau and Jacob. [19]These are the descendants of Isaac, son of Abraham; Abraham begot Isaac. [20]Isaac was forty years old when he married Rebekah, the daughter of Bethuel the Aramean of Paddan-aram and the sister of Laban the Aramean. [21]Isaac entreated the LORD on behalf of his wife, since she was sterile. The LORD heard his entreaty, and his wife Rebekah became pregnant.

THE ANCESTRAL STORY
PART 2: ISAAC AND REBEKAH
Genesis 25:19–28:9

25:19-28 The births of Esau and Jacob

The stories about Isaac are far fewer than those about Abraham. Many of them are incorporated into the narratives about his father Abraham and his sons Jacob and Esau. The Isaac account continues the theme of divine promise of descendants and land. In the narrative the betrothal and barren mother type scenes reappear, as does the wife-sister motif. In addition, we meet here another motif that occurs throughout Genesis: that of the younger before the older. We will discuss these as we come to them in the Isaac stories.

After a brief genealogical note we learn that Rebekah, like Sarah before her, is sterile—an immediate threat to the promise, just as in the Abraham and Sarah saga. This time the childlessness is quickly overcome when Isaac prays to God and Rebekah becomes pregnant. Her pregnancy, however, is not without difficulty. She carries twins who jostle each other in the womb, making her pregnancy very uncomfortable. Rebekah brings her concern to the Lord, and the divine response confirms that she will bear twins who will father opposing nations; indeed the tension between them has already begun in Rebekah's womb. The Lord informs Rebekah that the older will serve the younger, an unusual arrangement in ancient Near Eastern families.

The story follows the plot of the barren mother type scene: the childless Rebekah has a son (Jacob) and takes steps to insure his success. This account follows the request model, in which Isaac asks God for a son for his wife, and the Lord grants his request. The story alludes to the competition model

²²But the children jostled each other in the womb so much that she exclaimed, "If it is like this, why go on living!" She went to consult the Lord, ²³and the Lord answered her:

> Two nations are in your womb,
> two peoples are separating
> while still within you;
> But one will be stronger than the other,
> and the older will serve the younger.

²⁴When the time of her delivery came, there were twins in her womb. ²⁵The first to emerge was reddish, and his whole body was like a hairy mantle; so they named him Esau. ²⁶Next his brother came out, gripping Esau's heel; so he was named Jacob. Isaac was sixty years old when they were born.

²⁷When the boys grew up, Esau became a skillful hunter, a man of the open country; whereas Jacob was a simple man, who stayed among the tents. ²⁸Isaac preferred Esau, because he was fond of game; but Rebekah preferred Jacob. ²⁹Once, when Jacob was cooking a stew, Esau came in from the open country,

---

as well, in the struggle between the two boys. Rebekah does not have a rival wife, but she carries the strife between her two sons even before they are born. The divine response to her prayer in the face of her difficult pregnancy explains the conflict, confirms that it is of divine origin, and announces the reversal of roles between the two brothers. This divine word forms the backdrop for all Rebekah's actions to ensure the success of her younger son Jacob.

In addition, the story alludes to the promise model in the divine explanation to Rebekah while her sons are still in her womb. The threefold promise announces that the tension between the two boys will continue throughout their lives: they will form two different nations; they will struggle for power; and their roles in the family will be reversed.

When the twins are born, Esau comes first, followed by his brother Jacob. Their names foreshadow the defining characteristics of each: Esau is hairy and reddish, and Jacob is the heel-gripper. With their contrasting personalities the two appeal to different parents: Esau the impetuous outdoorsman is his father's favorite while his mother prefers Jacob, the methodical and conniving tent-dweller.

25:29-34 Esau sells his birthright

The first illustration of the boys' contrasting personalities comes when Jacob is preparing a stew. Esau refers to it as "red stuff"; the narrative calls it lentil stew (v. 34). We recall that when Esau was born he was reddish,

famished. [30]He said to Jacob, "Let me gulp down some of that red stuff; I am famished." That is why he was called Edom. [31]But Jacob replied, "First sell me your right as firstborn." [32]"Look," said Esau, "I am on the point of dying. What good is the right as firstborn to me?" [33]But Jacob said, "Swear to me first!" So he sold Jacob his right as firstborn under oath. [34]Jacob then gave him some bread and the lentil stew; and Esau ate, drank, got up, and went his way. So Esau treated his right as firstborn with disdain.

Isaac and Abimelech. [1]There was 26 a famine in the land, distinct from the earlier one that had occurred in the days of Abraham, and Isaac went down to Abimelech, king of the Philistines in Gerar. [2]The LORD appeared to him and said: Do not go down to Egypt, but camp in this land wherever I tell you. [3]Sojourn in this land, and I will be with you and bless you; for to you and your descendants I will give all these lands, in fulfillment of the oath that I swore to your father Abraham. [4]I will make your descendants as numerous as the stars in the sky, and I will give them all these lands, and in your descendants all the nations of the earth will find blessing— [5]this because Abraham obeyed me, keeping my mandate, my commandments, my ordinances, and my instructions.

[6]So Isaac settled in Gerar. [7]When the men of the place asked questions about his wife, he answered, "She is my sister."

---

probably a reference to a ruddy complexion (v. 25). Here the color of the stew attracts his attention; perhaps he thinks it contains blood, which would appeal to his hunter's tastes. In fact, the color comes from the lentils, which would appeal to a vegetarian.

Jacob seizes the opportunity to strike a bargain with his brother, and agrees to give him a bowl of stew in exchange for Esau's birthright. This is a hard bargain, considering the inequality of the tradeoff. It highlights both Jacob's scheming personality and Esau's utter lack of concern for a matter with long-term implications. It also foreshadows Jacob's deception of his father Isaac when he arranges to receive the blessing intended for his brother Esau in chapter 27.

26:1-35 Rebekah endangered

The narrative returns to Isaac, who must care for his family in the midst of a famine. Just as his father did previously, Isaac prepares to migrate in search of food. Egypt is not an option for him because the Lord insists that he stay in the land of promise. At this point the Lord repeats to Isaac the promise of descendants, a nation, and land that was made so many times to Abraham. Instead of going to Egypt, Isaac travels to Gerar, as Abraham did during the second famine (ch. 20).

He was afraid that, if he called her his wife, the men of the place would kill him on account of Rebekah, since she was beautiful. ⁸But when they had been there for a long time, Abimelech, king of the Philistines, looked out of a window and saw Isaac fondling his wife Rebekah. ⁹He called for Isaac and said: "She must certainly be your wife! How could you have said, 'She is my sister'?" Isaac replied, "I thought I might lose my life on her account." ¹⁰"How could you have done this to us!" exclaimed Abimelech. "It would have taken very little for one of the people to lie with your wife, and so you would have brought guilt upon us!" ¹¹Abimelech then commanded all the people: "Anyone who maltreats this man or his wife shall be put to death."

¹²Isaac sowed a crop in that region and reaped a hundredfold the same year. Since the Lord blessed him, ¹³he became richer and richer all the time, until he was very wealthy. ¹⁴He acquired flocks and herds, and a great work force, and so the Philistines became envious of him. ¹⁵The Philistines had stopped up and filled with dirt all the wells that his father's servants had dug back in the days of his father Abraham. ¹⁶So Abimelech said to Isaac, "Go away from us; you have become far too numerous for us." ¹⁷Isaac left there and camped in the Wadi Gerar where he stayed. ¹⁸Isaac reopened the wells which his father's servants had dug back in the days of his father Abraham and which the Philistines had stopped up after Abraham's death; he gave them names like those that his father had given them. ¹⁹But when Isaac's servants dug in the wadi and reached spring water in their well,

---

In verse 6 the wife-sister motif appears again, in the same location, Gerar, that was problematic for Abraham and Sarah in chapter 20. This time there is no prior arrangement between Isaac and Rebekah; the narrative simply tells us that Isaac identifies Rebekah as his sister when the men of Gerar approach him because of her. (Like Sarah, Rebekah is beautiful.) Isaac's first concern is for his own safety, as was Abraham's before him; he fears for his life at the hands of the inhabitants of Gerar.

This time there is no attempt on the part of Abimelech the king to take Rebekah; instead, he happens to see Isaac and Rebekah enjoying each other as husband and wife. The Hebrew word that describes their action comes from the same root as the word "Isaac," which means "laughter" and recalls the joy of Isaac's parents at his birth. But the moment creates the opposite of joy for Abimelech when he realizes that Rebekah and Isaac are husband and wife. The conversation that follows between Abimelech and Isaac shows that Isaac's fears are in vain. Abimelech has no intention of violating Isaac's wife, and he forbids his people to mistreat either of them. This mandate confirms Isaac's earlier fear: the people might indeed have

20the shepherds of Gerar argued with Isaac's shepherds, saying, "The water belongs to us!" So he named the well Esek, because they had quarreled there. 21Then they dug another well, and they argued over that one too; so he named it Sitnah. 22So he moved on from there and dug still another well, but over this one they did not argue. He named it Rehoboth, and said, "Because the LORD has now given us ample room, we shall flourish in the land."

23From there Isaac went up to Beersheba. 24The same night the LORD appeared to him and said: I am the God of Abraham, your father. Do not fear, for I am with you. I will bless you and multiply your descendants for the sake of Abraham, my servant. 25So Isaac built an altar there and invoked the LORD by name. After he had pitched his tent there, Isaac's servants began to dig a well nearby.

26Then Abimelech came to him from Gerar, with Ahuzzath, his councilor, and Phicol, the general of his army. 27Isaac asked them, "Why have you come to me, since you hate me and have driven me away from you?" 28They answered: "We clearly see that the LORD has been with you, so we thought: let there be a sworn agreement between our two sides— between you and us. Let us make a covenant with you: 29you shall do no harm to us, just as we have not maltreated you, but have always acted kindly toward you and have let you depart in peace. So now, may you be blessed by the LORD!" 30Isaac then made a feast for them, and they ate and drank. 31Early the next

violated Rebekah. It also highlights Isaac's duplicity: if the people had violated Rebekah, it would have been Isaac's fault.

The next episode describes a second incident when tensions arise between Isaac and Abimelech. This time the cause is Isaac's hugely successful farming in Gerar. In an effort to drive him away the Philistines stop up the wells that Abraham dug, and Abimelech directly asks him to leave. Isaac moves to the area where Abraham stayed (21:34), re-digs his father's wells, and discovers a spring in one of them. This valuable water source causes a new round of conflict, so Isaac moves again and digs other wells. These incidents highlight the scarcity of water in the region, and the desire of each family to protect its water sources, particularly during a famine.

Eventually (v. 23) Isaac returns to Beer-sheba, where he had lived with his father Abraham. Here the Lord appears to him and repeats the promise of descendants. Isaac builds an altar to mark the place where the Lord appeared, just as his father had done. After praying to the Lord, he sets about digging a well. Again he must reckon with Abimelech, who recognizes the power that Isaac has accrued by his economic success. In verse 26 Abimelech and his men ask for a nonaggression pact between the two peoples. Isaac

morning they exchanged oaths. Then Isaac sent them on their way, and they departed from him in peace.

³²That same day Isaac's servants came and informed him about the well they had been digging; they told him, "We have reached water!" ³³He called it Shibah; hence the name of the city is Beer-sheba to this day. ³⁴When Esau was forty years old, he married Judith, daughter of Beeri the Hittite, and Basemath, daughter of Elon the Hivite. ³⁵But they became a source of bitterness to Isaac and Rebekah.

27 Jacob's Deception. ¹When Isaac was so old that his eyesight had failed him, he called his older son Esau and said to him, "My son!" "Here I am!" he replied. ²Isaac then said, "Now I have grown old. I do not know when I might die. ³So now take your hunting gear—your quiver and bow—and go out into the open country to hunt some game for me. ⁴Then prepare for me a dish in the way I like, and bring it to me to eat, so that I may bless you before I die."

⁵Rebekah had been listening while Isaac was speaking to his son Esau. So when Esau went out into the open country to hunt some game for his father, ⁶Rebekah said to her son Jacob, "Listen! I heard your father tell your brother Esau, ⁷'Bring me some game and prepare a dish for me to eat, that I may bless you with the Lord's approval before I die.' ⁸Now, my son, obey me in what I am about to order you. ⁹Go to the flock and get me two choice young goats so that with these I might prepare a dish for your father in the way he likes. ¹⁰Then bring it to your father to eat, that he may bless you before he dies." ¹¹But Jacob said to his mother Rebekah, "But my brother Esau is a hairy man and I am smooth-skinned! ¹²Suppose my father feels me? He will think I am making fun of him, and I will bring on myself a curse instead of a blessing." ¹³His mother, however, replied: "Let any curse against you, my son, fall on me! Just obey me. Go and get me the young goats."

¹⁴So Jacob went and got them and brought them to his mother, and she prepared a dish in the way his father liked. ¹⁵Rebekah then took the best clothes of her older son Esau that she had in the

agrees, and they make a formal agreement. A brief genealogical note follows in verse 34, listing Esau's marriages to a Hittite woman and a Hivite woman, a cause of bitterness to his parents. It foreshadows Rebekah's determination that Jacob, not Esau, will receive Isaac's blessing now that Esau has married outside the family.

27:1-45 Isaac blesses Jacob

The saga continues as Isaac arranges to bestow his blessing on his son before he dies, like Abraham before him. This episode, in which Rebekah helps Jacob to usurp the blessing intended for Esau, takes place in seven steps, permeated by the motif of younger-older.

house, and gave them to her younger son Jacob to wear; [16]and with the goat-skins she covered up his hands and the hairless part of his neck. [17]Then she gave her son Jacob the dish and the bread she had prepared.

[18]Going to his father, Jacob said, "Father!" "Yes?" replied Isaac. "Which of my sons are you?" [19]Jacob answered his father: "I am Esau, your firstborn. I did as you told me. Please sit up and eat some of my game, so that you may bless me." [20]But Isaac said to his son, "How did you get it so quickly, my son?" He answered, "The LORD, your God, directed me." [21]Isaac then said to Jacob, "Come closer, my son, that I may feel you, to learn whether you really are my son Esau or not." [22]So Jacob moved up closer to his father. When Isaac felt him, he said, "Although the voice is Jacob's, the hands are Esau's." [23](He failed to identify him because his hands were hairy, like those of his brother Esau; so he blessed him.) [24]Again Isaac said, "Are you really my son Esau?" And Jacob said, "I am." [25]Then Isaac said, "Serve me, my son, and let me eat of the game so that I may bless you." Jacob served it to him, and Isaac ate; he brought him wine, and he drank. [26]Finally his father Isaac said to him, "Come closer, my son, and kiss me." [27]As Jacob went up to kiss him, Isaac smelled the fragrance of his clothes. With that, he blessed him, saying,

> "Ah, the fragrance of my son
>   is like the fragrance of a field
>   that the LORD has blessed!
> [28]May God give to you
>   of the dew of the heavens
> And of the fertility of the earth
>   abundance of grain and wine.
> [29]May peoples serve you,
>   and nations bow down to you;
> Be master of your brothers,
>   and may your mother's sons
>   bow down to you.
> Cursed be those who curse you,
>   and blessed be those who bless
>   you."

The first step (vv. 1-4) involves Isaac and Esau. We learn that Isaac's eyesight is failing, and he instructs his son Esau to hunt game with which to prepare him a meal, so Esau might receive his father's blessing. The formality of the request is evident in several details: first, Esau responds with "Here I am!" the formal acknowledgment of readiness and willingness. In addition, the meal his father requests has a ritual connotation; here it suggests a formal ceremony for bestowing the blessing.

The second step (vv. 5-17) involves the other two people, Rebekah and Jacob. Rebekah repeats what she heard Isaac say to Esau, adding the solemn words, "with the Lord's approval." She quickly formulates a plan and explains it to Jacob. She brushes aside his hesitation because she remembers the Lord's words, "the older will serve the younger," when the twins were still in her womb (25:23). They both make the necessary preparations, and Rebekah sends him in to his father.

³⁰Jacob had scarcely left his father after Isaac had finished blessing him, when his brother Esau came back from his hunt. ³¹Then he too prepared a dish, and bringing it to his father, he said, "Let my father sit up and eat some of his son's game, that you may then give me your blessing." ³²His father Isaac asked him, "Who are you?" He said, "I am your son, your firstborn son, Esau." ³³Isaac trembled greatly. "Who was it, then," he asked, "that hunted game and brought it to me? I ate it all just before you came, and I blessed him. Now he is blessed!" ³⁴As he heard his father's words, Esau burst into loud, bitter sobbing and said, "Father, bless me too!" ³⁵When Isaac said, "Your brother came here by a ruse and carried off your blessing," ³⁶Esau exclaimed, "He is well named Jacob, is he not! He has supplanted me twice! First he took away my right as firstborn, and now he has taken away my blessing." Then he said, "Have you not saved a blessing for me?" ³⁷Isaac replied to Esau: "I have already appointed him your master, and I have assigned to him all his kindred as his servants; besides, I have sustained him with grain and wine. What then can I do for you, my son?" ³⁸But Esau said to his father, "Have you only one blessing,

The third step (vv. 18-29) takes place between Isaac and Jacob. Jacob lies to his father in order to receive the blessing intended for his brother. Because Isaac is losing his eyesight, he does not recognize Jacob, but questions the voice that sounds like Esau's. He blesses Jacob, assuring him of prosperity, political and military power, and divine protection.

The fourth step (vv. 30-41) brings together Isaac and Esau for the second time, when Esau returns after making the preparations his father directed. He and Isaac both realize what has happened, but it is too late to retract the blessing that has been given to Jacob. When Esau pleads for a blessing for himself, Isaac responds with the blessing of prosperity. He then announces that Esau will live a life of violence and subservience to his brother until he breaks free of him. Esau makes up his mind to kill his brother once their father is dead.

The fifth step (vv. 42-45) brings together Jacob and Rebekah for the second time. She urges him to leave at once and go to her brother Laban rather than risk being killed by Esau. She fears losing both of her sons at once: Jacob if Esau kills him, and Esau if he is condemned for killing his brother.

The sixth step (v. 46) takes place between Rebekah and Isaac. Rather than admit to her husband that she masterminded the deceitful events, she picks up the theme of 26:34-35: Esau's marriages outside the family have brought grief to his parents. Rebekah wants assurance that Jacob will marry within

father? Bless me too, father!" and Esau wept aloud. [39]His father Isaac said in response:

> "See, far from the fertile earth
>> will be your dwelling;
>> far from the dew of the heavens
>>> above!
> [40]By your sword you will live,
>> and your brother you will serve;
> But when you become restless,
>> you will throw off his yoke from
>>> your neck."

[41]Esau bore a grudge against Jacob because of the blessing his father had given him. Esau said to himself, "Let the time of mourning for my father come, so that I may kill my brother Jacob." [42]When Rebekah got news of what her older son Esau had in mind, she summoned her younger son Jacob and said to him: "Listen! Your brother Esau intends to get his revenge by killing you. [43]So now, my son, obey me: flee at once to my brother Laban in Haran, [44]and stay with him a while until your brother's fury subsides—[45]until your brother's anger against you subsides and he forgets what you did to him. Then I will send for you and bring you back. Why should I lose both of you in a single day?"

the family, to avoid further sorrow. Her request to send Jacob away has the added advantage of protecting the promise of children and land.

The seventh step (28:1-5) brings together Isaac and Jacob for the second time. Isaac formally sends Jacob to Rebekah's brother Laban to find a wife for himself. He repeats to Jacob the divine promise of land, children, and a nation in the name of his father Abraham, and Jacob sets out on the journey. This is the first time Jacob receives the promise; it comes from his father Isaac.

The episode brings out the deceptive aspect of Jacob's character even more strongly than the incident with the stew. Here Jacob deliberately lies to his father (at the encouragement of his mother) in order to get what he wants. It is true that the Lord intends for Jacob to win out over his brother. The means to this end are questionable, though, and Jacob's deception will come back to haunt him. The incident also highlights the extent of Esau's bitterness at his own situation. He arranges to marry one of Ishmael's daughters, to exacerbate his parents' displeasure with him. In addition, in this scene Isaac passes on the promise of descendants, land, and nation to his son Jacob. The event marks the successful completion of Isaac's primary role: he has carried the promise forward to the next generation and entrusted it to the son chosen by God.

Here the narrative leaves Isaac and focuses on Jacob until it announces Isaac's death in 35:27-29. We learn of Jacob's journey to his uncle Laban,

Jacob Sent to Laban. [46]Rebekah said to Isaac: "I am disgusted with life because of the Hittite women. If Jacob also should marry a Hittite woman, a native of the land, like these women, why should I live?"

28 [1]Isaac therefore summoned Jacob and blessed him, charging him: "You shall not marry a Canaanite woman! [2]Go now to Paddan-aram, to the home of your mother's father Bethuel, and there choose a wife for yourself from among the daughters of Laban, your mother's brother. [3]May God Almighty bless you and make you fertile, multiply you that you may become an assembly of peoples. [4]May God extend to you and your descendants the blessing of Abraham, so that you may gain possession of the land where you are residing, which he assigned to Abra-

ham." [5]Then Isaac sent Jacob on his way; he went to Paddan-aram, to Laban, son of Bethuel the Aramean, and brother of Rebekah, the mother of Jacob and Esau.

[6]Esau noted that Isaac had blessed Jacob when he sent him to Paddan-aram to get himself a wife there, and that, as he gave him his blessing, he charged him, "You shall not marry a Canaanite woman," [7]and that Jacob had obeyed his father and mother and gone to Paddan-aram. [8]Esau realized how displeasing the Canaanite women were to his father Isaac, [9]so Esau went to Ishmael, and in addition to the wives he had, married Mahalath, the daughter of Abraham's son Ishmael and sister of Nebaioth.

Jacob's Dream at Bethel. [10]Jacob departed from Beer-sheba and proceeded toward Haran. [11]When he came upon a

---

his marriages and the births of his children, the tensions between him and Laban, and his meeting with his brother Esau before he returns home. Twice on his journey, once on the way to Haran and once on the way back home, he encounters God.

THE ANCESTRAL STORY
PART 3: JACOB AND HIS WIVES

Genesis 28:10–36:43

28:10-22 Jacob at Bethel

Just as in the report of the servant's journey to find a wife for Isaac, here we learn only the essentials of Jacob's trip, except for one event that takes place along the way. He stops for the night, apparently out in the open, at a place that has something special about it. There he has a dream in which the Lord gives Jacob the promise of descendants and land. Jacob received that promise from his father before setting out on his journey. Now he receives it directly from God. The deity's name is "LORD," the God of his

certain place, he stopped there for the night, since the sun had already set. Taking one of the stones at the place, he put it under his head and lay down in that place. ¹²Then he had a dream: a stairway rested on the ground, with its top reaching to the heavens; and God's angels were going up and down on it. ¹³And there was the LORD standing beside him and saying: I am the LORD, the God of Abraham your father and the God of Isaac; the land on which you are lying I will give to you and your descendants. ¹⁴Your descendants will be like the dust of the earth, and through them you will spread to the west and the east, to the north and the south. In you and your descendants all the families of the earth will find blessing. ¹⁵I am with you and will protect you wherever you go, and bring you back to this land. I will never leave you until I have done what I promised you.

¹⁶When Jacob awoke from his sleep, he said, "Truly, the LORD is in this place and I did not know it!" ¹⁷He was afraid and said: "How awesome this place is! This is nothing else but the house of God, the gateway to heaven!" ¹⁸Early the next morning Jacob took the stone that he had put under his head, set it up as a sacred pillar, and poured oil on top of it. ¹⁹He named that place Bethel, whereas the former name of the town had been Luz.

²⁰Jacob then made this vow: "If God will be with me and protect me on this journey I am making and give me food to eat and clothes to wear, ²¹and I come back safely to my father's house, the LORD will be my God. ²²This stone that I have set up as a sacred pillar will be the

---

father and grandfather. This identification makes it clear that, even though Jacob is probably sleeping at a shrine to a local deity, the God who speaks to him there is not the local god but the God who has cared for his family for several generations.

The Lord reiterates the promises of land, descendants, a nation, and divine blessing. When Jacob realizes that he has met the Lord he takes the stone pillow, sets it up vertically, and pours oil on it to designate it as holy because his head rested on it during his revelatory dream. It is thus a witness to the event (see Josh 24:27). Jacob does not build an altar, as his grandfather Abraham did to mark the places where he met the Lord. Instead, he consecrates the stone, then formally accepts the terms of his encounter with God. He names the place Bethel, or House of God, the place near where Abraham once built an altar (12:8).

This story has an element of the E strand in which dreams are an important means of divine communication with humans. Dreaming is an act beyond human control, which takes place in a realm we cannot access by our own efforts. We often gain valuable insights while dreaming; ancient people understood these as revelations from God.

house of God. Of everything you give me, I will return a tenth part to you without fail."

29 **Arrival in Haran.** [1]After Jacob resumed his journey, he came to the land of the Kedemites. [2]Looking about, he saw a well in the open country, with three flocks of sheep huddled near it, for flocks were watered from that well. A large stone covered the mouth of the well. [3]When all the shepherds were assembled there they would roll the stone away from the mouth of the well and water the sheep. Then they would put the stone back again in its place over the mouth of the well.

[4]Jacob said to them, "My brothers, where are you from?" "We are from Haran," they replied. [5]Then he asked them, "Do you know Laban, son of Nahor?" "We do," they answered. [6]He inquired further, "Is he well?" "He is," they answered; "and here comes his daughter Rachel with the sheep." [7]Then he said: "There is still much daylight left; it is hardly the time to bring the animals home. Water the sheep, and then continue pasturing them." [8]They replied, "We cannot until all the shepherds are here to roll the stone away from the mouth of the well; then can we water the flocks."

29:1-30 Jacob's marriages

The narrative resumes with Jacob's arrival in the general area of his uncle's home. The plot follows the elements of the betrothal type scene. By looking at those elements we can see the story unfold, and can also compare and contrast Jacob's experience with that of Abraham's servant when he went to Haran in search of a wife for Isaac. Jacob arrives at a well that is covered with a large stone, surrounded by several flocks of sheep. Shepherds are with them; when Jacob asks if they know Laban he learns that Laban's daughter Rachel is arriving at that moment with her father's flock.

These details set the stage for a very different experience from that of Abraham's servant who came with a large retinue of gifts for Laban and his family. Jacob comes on the one hand as one sent by God and on the other as a fugitive. He brings nothing with him. Instead, Jacob offers his services, the first of which is to remove the stone from the well. He manages the stone singlehandedly, even though it is huge, because he is thrilled at the sight of Rachel. It is not clear whether he is responding to the sight of a relative or to an attractive young woman; perhaps to both. Then Jacob, instead of asking for water and receiving it from the woman, offers to water Laban's sheep. He further expresses his delight by tearfully kissing Rachel, a gesture of delight and gratitude at meeting his relative (v. 11).

⁹While he was still talking with them, Rachel arrived with her father's sheep, for she was the one who tended them. ¹⁰As soon as Jacob saw Rachel, the daughter of his mother's brother Laban, and the sheep of Laban, he went up, rolled the stone away from the mouth of the well, and watered Laban's sheep. ¹¹Then Jacob kissed Rachel and wept aloud. ¹²Jacob told Rachel that he was her father's relative, Rebekah's son. So she ran to tell her father. ¹³When Laban heard the news about Jacob, his sister's son, he ran to meet him. After embracing and kissing him, he brought him to his house. Jacob then repeated to Laban all these things, ¹⁴and Laban said to him, "You are indeed my bone and my flesh."

Marriage to Leah and Rachel. After Jacob had stayed with him a full month, ¹⁵Laban said to him: "Should you serve me for nothing just because you are a relative of mine? Tell me what your wages should be." ¹⁶Now Laban had two daughters; the older was called Leah, the younger Rachel. ¹⁷Leah had dull eyes, but Rachel was shapely and beautiful. ¹⁸Because Jacob loved Rachel, he answered, "I will serve you seven years for your younger daughter Rachel." ¹⁹Laban replied, "It is better to give her to you

True to the type scene, Rachel hurries to tell her father of Jacob's arrival. He greets the visitor and invites him into his home. Then the narrative tells us only that Jacob told the story of his adventures; it does not repeat Jacob's words as Abraham's servant did.

The arrangements for the betrothal proceed much more slowly here than with Abraham's servant. A month passes before the subject comes up, and then Jacob mentions it in response to Laban's offer to pay Jacob for his services. Jacob offers to work for Laban for seven years in exchange for Rachel's hand (29:18). (Jacob must work for the privilege of marrying Laban's daughter because he does not bring gifts with him, as did Abraham's servant.) The narrative points out that Rachel is the younger of Laban's two daughters, bringing into play the younger-older motif. Jacob meets his match when Laban gives him his older daughter Leah in marriage instead of Rachel, then falls back on ancient tradition as his excuse for the deceitful arrangement. He assures Jacob that, after the customary seven days of celebration of the first marriage, Jacob may work seven more years for Rachel, and Jacob agrees.

Then the story picks up the barren mother type scene, and the competition model begins to unfold. Two women are married to the same husband; one has children and the other does not. The narrative highlights the divine action on behalf of Leah for her unfavored status. Leah bears four sons:

than to another man. Stay with me." ²⁰So Jacob served seven years for Rachel, yet they seemed to him like a few days because of his love for her.

²¹Then Jacob said to Laban, "Give me my wife, that I may consummate my marriage with her, for my term is now completed." ²²So Laban invited all the local inhabitants and gave a banquet. ²³At nightfall he took his daughter Leah and brought her to Jacob, and he consummated the marriage with her. ²⁴Laban assigned his maidservant Zilpah to his daughter Leah as her maidservant. ²⁵In the morning, there was Leah! So Jacob said to Laban: "How could you do this to me! Was it not for Rachel that I served you? Why did you deceive me?" ²⁶Laban replied, "It is not the custom in our country to give the younger daughter before the firstborn. ²⁷Finish the bridal week for this one, and then the

other will also be given to you in return for another seven years of service with me."

²⁸Jacob did so. He finished the bridal week for the one, and then Laban gave him his daughter Rachel as a wife. ²⁹Laban assigned his maidservant Bilhah to his daughter Rachel as her maidservant. ³⁰Jacob then consummated his marriage with Rachel also, and he loved her more than Leah. Thus he served Laban another seven years.

Jacob's Children. ³¹When the LORD saw that Leah was unloved, he made her fruitful, while Rachel was barren. ³²Leah conceived and bore a son, and she named him Reuben; for she said, "It means, 'The LORD saw my misery; surely now my husband will love me.'" ³³She conceived again and bore a son, and said, "It means, 'The LORD heard that I was unloved,' and therefore he has given

Reuben, Simeon, Levi, and Judah. The names she gives the boys reflect her situation as the unloved wife. The note that she then stops bearing sons foreshadows further difficulties to come.

The request model of the barren mother type scene overlaps with the competition model when Rachel pleads desperately with Jacob to give her children in 30:1. But Jacob does not accept responsibility for her childlessness, and reminds her that children are gifts from God. In her despair she offers her maid Bilhah to Jacob, just as Sarah offered Hagar to Abraham. Rachel arranges that Bilhah will bear surrogate children for her; she clarifies her own maternal status by arranging to hold Bilhah's children on her own knees. The act of holding a child on one's knees legitimates him as the son of that parent (see 48:12 and 50:23). Bilhah bears two sons, whom Rachel names Dan and Naphtali, referring to the competition between her and Leah.

Not to be outdone, Leah then gives her maid Zilpah to Jacob (v. 9). Zilpah bears two sons, giving them names that suggest Leah's own good fortune:

me this one also"; so she named him Simeon. [34]Again she conceived and bore a son, and she said, "Now at last my husband will become attached to me, since I have now borne him three sons"; that is why she named him Levi. [35]Once more she conceived and bore a son, and she said, "This time I will give thanks to the LORD"; therefore she named him Judah. Then she stopped bearing children.

◄ 30 [1]When Rachel saw that she had not borne children to Jacob, she became envious of her sister. She said to Jacob, "Give me children or I shall die!" [2]Jacob became angry with Rachel and said, "Can I take the place of God, who has denied you the fruit of the womb?" [3]She replied, "Here is my maidservant Bilhah. Have intercourse with her, and let her give birth on my knees, so that I too may have children through her." [4]So she gave him her maidservant Bilhah as wife, and Jacob had intercourse with her. [5]When Bilhah conceived and bore a son for Jacob, [6]Rachel said, "God has vindicated me; indeed he has heeded my plea and given me a son." Therefore she named him Dan. [7]Rachel's maidservant Bilhah conceived again and bore a second son for Jacob, [8]and Rachel said, "I have wrestled strenuously with my sister, and I have prevailed." So she named him Naphtali.

[9]When Leah saw that she had ceased to bear children, she took her maidservant Zilpah and gave her to Jacob as wife. [10]So Leah's maidservant Zilpah bore a son for Jacob. [11]Leah then said, "What good luck!" So she named him Gad. [12]Then Leah's maidservant Zilpah bore a second son to Jacob; [13]and Leah

---

Gad and Asher. Jacob now has eight sons, but none by his favored wife Rachel. Leah's son Reuben offers his mother some mandrakes, known for their aphrodisiac qualities. When Rachel asks for some of them she learns of Leah's bitterness at her own unloved status, so Rachel makes a deal: Rachel will have the mandrakes, but Leah will spend the night with Jacob. Leah bears two more sons, whom she names Issachar and Zebulun, reflecting her awkward relationship with Jacob. The narrative then reports that she also bears a daughter whom she names Dinah. No interpretation of her name or other details are given about Dinah.

Only after Jacob already has ten sons and a daughter does Rachel bear a son (v. 22). The narrative specifies that God remembers her; that is, God focuses attention on her. She bears Joseph, whose name suggests both removing her past shame and adding hope and joy to her future. By now eleven sons are born to Jacob and his four women: six to Leah, two to each of the two maids Bilhah and Zilpah, and one to Rachel. In addition he has one daughter by Leah. Throughout the narrative, all the women compete with one another for Jacob's love and for children. While the humans strive

said, "What good fortune, because women will call me fortunate!" So she named him Asher.

¹⁴One day, during the wheat harvest, Reuben went out and came upon some mandrakes in the field which he brought home to his mother Leah. Rachel said to Leah, "Please give me some of your son's mandrakes." ¹⁵Leah replied, "Was it not enough for you to take away my husband, that you must now take my son's mandrakes too?" Rachel answered, "In that case Jacob may lie with you tonight in exchange for your son's mandrakes." ¹⁶That evening, when Jacob came in from the field, Leah went out to meet him. She said, "You must have intercourse with me, because I have hired you with my son's mandrakes." So that night he lay with her, ¹⁷and God listened to Leah; she conceived and bore a fifth son to Jacob. ¹⁸Leah then said, "God has given me my wages for giving my maidservant to my husband"; so she named him Issachar. ¹⁹Leah conceived again and bore a sixth son to Jacob; ²⁰and

Leah said, "God has brought me a precious gift. This time my husband will honor me, because I have borne him six sons"; so she named him Zebulun. ²¹Afterwards she gave birth to a daughter, and she named her Dinah.

²²Then God remembered Rachel. God listened to her and made her fruitful. ²³She conceived and bore a son, and she said, "God has removed my disgrace." ²⁴She named him Joseph, saying, "May the LORD add another son for me!"

Jacob Outwits Laban. ²⁵After Rachel gave birth to Joseph, Jacob said to Laban: "Allow me to go to my own region and land. ²⁶Give me my wives and my children for whom I served you and let me go, for you know the service that I rendered you." ²⁷Laban answered him: "If you will please! I have learned through divination that the LORD has blessed me because of you." ²⁸He continued, "State the wages I owe you, and I will pay them." ²⁹Jacob replied: "You know what work I did for you and how well your livestock fared under my care; ³⁰the little

to control the situation, the narrative repeats frequently that it is God who gives children, assuring that the promise of descendants moves forward into the next generation.

30:25-43 Jacob tricks Laban

The story shifts back to the relationship between Jacob and his father-in-law Laban, and continues the motif of trickery that permeates the story of Jacob's marriage, his wives, and his children. After fourteen years of working for Laban in exchange for his two wives, he works for Laban six more years. By the end of the twenty years he has twelve children. In accordance with the divine promise to Jacob in his dream at Bethel to bring him back to his father's land (28:15), Jacob asks Laban's permission to return home.

you had before I came has grown into an abundance, since the LORD has blessed you in my company. Now, when can I do something for my own household as well?" ³¹Laban asked, "What should I give you?" Jacob answered: "You do not have to give me anything. If you do this thing for me, I will again pasture and tend your sheep. ³²Let me go through your whole flock today and remove from it every dark animal among the lambs and every spotted or speckled one among the goats. These will be my wages. ³³In the future, whenever you check on my wages, my honesty will testify for me: any animal that is not speckled or spotted among the goats, or dark among the lambs, got into my possession by theft!" ³⁴Laban said, "Very well. Let it be as you say."

³⁵That same day Laban removed the streaked and spotted he-goats and all the speckled and spotted she-goats, all those with some white on them, as well as every dark lamb, and he put them in the care of his sons. ³⁶Then he put a three days' journey between himself and Jacob, while Jacob was pasturing the rest of Laban's flock.

³⁷Jacob, however, got some fresh shoots of poplar, almond and plane trees, and he peeled white stripes in them by laying bare the white core of the shoots. ³⁸The shoots that he had peeled he then set upright in the watering troughs where the animals came to drink, so that they would be in front of them. When the animals were in heat as they came to drink, ³⁹the goats mated by the shoots, and so they gave birth to streaked, speckled and spotted young. ⁴⁰The sheep, on the other hand, Jacob kept apart, and he made these animals face the streaked or completely dark animals of Laban. Thus he produced flocks of his own, which he did not put with Laban's flock. ⁴¹Whenever the hardier animals were in heat, Jacob would set the shoots in the troughs in full view of these animals, so that they mated by the shoots; ⁴²but with the weaker animals he would not put the shoots there. So the feeble

---

The history of trickery between the two men leads us to suspect that the leave-taking will not be a simple one. They bargain for a fair arrangement: Laban realizes he will lose the valuable services of his son-in-law, who has been a blessing to him; and Jacob wants compensation for all his labor.

Jacob requests some of the animals from Laban's flocks: he asks for the dark sheep and the spotted goats. These animals, a small proportion of Laban's flocks, do not have the usual coloring. The arrangement will, however, be a foolproof way to determine which animals belong to which of the men. Laban separates the flocks according to color as agreed, and puts his sons in charge of those flocks destined for Jacob. Jacob alludes to their history of trickery when he asserts his honesty to Laban in verse 33. Laban moves his flocks a three-day journey away, but Jacob takes advantage

animals would go to Laban, but the hardy ones to Jacob. ⁴³So the man grew exceedingly prosperous, and he owned large flocks, male and female servants, camels, and donkeys.

31 **Flight from Laban.** ¹Jacob heard that Laban's sons were saying, "Jacob has taken everything that belonged to our father, and he has produced all this wealth from our father's property." ²Jacob perceived, too, that Laban's attitude toward him was not what it had previously been. ³Then the LORD said to Jacob: Return to the land of your ancestors, where you were born, and I will be with you.

⁴So Jacob sent for Rachel and Leah to meet him in the field where his flock was. ⁵There he said to them: "I have noticed that your father's attitude toward me is not as it was in the past; but the God of my father has been with me. ⁶You know well that with all my strength I served your father; ⁷yet your father cheated me and changed my wages ten times. God, however, did not let him do me any harm. ⁸Whenever your father said, 'The speckled animals will be your wages,' the entire flock would bear speckled young; whenever he said, 'The streaked animals will be your wages,' the entire flock would bear streaked young. ⁹So God took away your father's livestock and gave it to me. ¹⁰Once, during the flock's mating season, I had a dream in which I saw he-goats mating that were streaked, speckled and mottled. ¹¹In the dream God's angel said to me, 'Jacob!' and I replied, 'Here I am!' ¹²Then he said: 'Look up and see. All the he-goats that are mating are streaked, speckled and mottled, for I have seen all the things

of the isolation of those flocks to breed animals selectively, thus increasing the size and quality of his own flocks and other holdings (v. 43). Eventually he justifies this practice by attributing the idea to a dream (31:10-13), thus intimating that it is God's plan.

Jacob's scheme is so successful that he arouses the suspicion and mistrust of Laban and his sons. The time to depart has arrived, and once again we expect complications.

31:1-54 Jacob takes leave of Laban

After the payment for Jacob's services is settled and Jacob's continued presence with his uncle has become very problematic, Jacob receives word from the Lord to return home with the assurance of divine protection. But several more complications arise before the men finally separate. The plot reflects the duplicity, not only of Jacob and Laban, but also of Rachel. The episode takes place in five stages.

In the first, verses 1-16, Jacob sends for his two wives and explains that the Lord has instructed him to leave Laban and return to his own land in

93

An exceedingly prosperous flock of sheep, like that of Jacob

that Laban has been doing to you. ¹³I am the God of Bethel, where you anointed a sacred pillar and made a vow to me. Get up now! Leave this land and return to the land of your birth.'"

¹⁴Rachel and Leah answered him: "Do we still have an heir's portion in our father's house? ¹⁵Are we not regarded by him as outsiders? He not only sold us; he has even used up the money that he got for us! ¹⁶All the wealth that God took away from our father really belongs to us and our children. So do whatever God has told you." ¹⁷Jacob proceeded to put his children and wives on camels, ¹⁸and he drove off all his livestock and all the property he had acquired in Paddan-aram, to go to his father Isaac in the land of Canaan.

¹⁹Now Laban was away shearing his sheep, and Rachel had stolen her father's household images. ²⁰Jacob had hoodwinked Laban the Aramean by not tell-

ing him that he was going to flee. ²¹Thus he fled with all that he had. Once he was across the Euphrates, he headed for the hill country of Gilead.

²²On the third day, word came to Laban that Jacob had fled. ²³Taking his kinsmen with him, he pursued him for seven days until he caught up with him in the hill country of Gilead. ²⁴But that night God appeared to Laban the Aramean in a dream and said to him: Take care not to say anything to Jacob.

Jacob and Laban in Gilead. ²⁵When Laban overtook Jacob, Jacob's tents were pitched in the hill country; Laban also pitched his tents in the hill country of Gilead. ²⁶Laban said to Jacob, "How could you hoodwink me and carry off my daughters like prisoners of war? ²⁷Why did you dupe me by stealing away secretly? You did not tell me! I would have sent you off with joyful singing to the sound of tambourines and

fulfillment of the agreement made at Bethel. He gives a detailed description of the situation, putting his own actions in a good light and Laban's in a bad light. Both wives agree with Jacob that their father has been unfair in dealing, not only with Jacob, but also with them. It is unusual that the two are of one mind; their agreement expresses their bitterness at their father's treatment of them. They encourage Jacob to do as God instructs.

In the second, verses 17-21, the family flees. They depart while Laban is away, taking with them all Jacob acquired over the years. In addition, Rachel steals her father's household gods. The reason for the theft is not clear: perhaps she wants simply to deprive him of them, or perhaps to use them for her own benefit, either by claiming them as an inheritance or by using them for religious purposes. In 27:43 Rebekah insisted that Jacob flee from his father's house; now he flees from his father-in-law's house.

In the third, verses 22-35, Laban learns that the party has fled and sets out in pursuit. After seven days, as he nears the fugitives, he has a dream

harps. [28]You did not even allow me a parting kiss to my daughters and grandchildren! Now what you have done makes no sense. [29]I have it in my power to harm all of you; but last night the God of your father said to me, 'Take care not to say anything to Jacob!' [30]Granted that you had to leave because you were longing for your father's house, why did you steal my gods?" [31]Jacob replied to Laban, "I was frightened at the thought that you might take your daughters away from me by force. [32]As for your gods, the one you find them with shall not remain alive! If, with our kinsmen looking on, you identify anything here as belonging to you, take it." Jacob had no idea that Rachel had stolen the household images.

[33]Laban then went in and searched Jacob's tent and Leah's tent, as well as the tents of the two maidservants; but he did not find them. Leaving Leah's tent, he went into Rachel's. [34]Meanwhile Rachel had taken the household images, put them inside the camel's saddlebag, and seated herself upon them. When Laban had rummaged through her whole tent without finding them, [35]she said to her father, "Do not let my lord be angry that I cannot rise in your presence; I am having my period." So, despite his search, he did not find the household images.

[36]Jacob, now angered, confronted Laban and demanded, "What crime or offense have I committed that you should hound me? [37]Now that you have

warning him not to interfere with Jacob. He confronts his son-in-law, accusing him of deceit and kidnapping. He bemoans his lost opportunity to give a proper farewell to his daughters and grandchildren, and then refers to the stolen household gods. Laban's complaint is filled with irony in light of his own treatment of Jacob from the time they first met. Jacob knows nothing of the stolen household gods, and assures Laban that he may have anything he finds that belongs to him.

Laban immediately begins to search the tents of each member of the party, saving Rachel's until last. She is ready for him: she had hidden the statues in a camel cushion, a combination saddle and storage box that is placed on a camel to provide seating and storage for the rider. She sits on the camel cushion, and protests that she cannot get up because she is menstruating. This adds to the irony of the situation: Rachel will not stand up to allow her father to search for the idols; in fact, he ought not to be in her presence under pain of defilement (Lev 15:19-23); but she defiles the idols by sitting on them in her claimed state of ritual uncleanness while at the same time protecting them from harm. Her action suggests that she herself does not believe the statues possess any power; otherwise she would treat them with respect. She accomplishes her purpose, however: Laban gives

rummaged through all my things, what have you found from your household belongings? Produce it here before your kinsmen and mine, and let them decide between the two of us.

[38]"In the twenty years that I was under you, no ewe or she-goat of yours ever miscarried, and I have never eaten rams of your flock. [39]I never brought you an animal torn by wild beasts; I made good the loss myself. You held me responsible for anything stolen by day or night. [40]Often the scorching heat devoured me by day, and the frost by night, while sleep fled from my eyes! [41]Of the twenty years that I have now spent in your household, I served you fourteen years for your two daughters and six years for your flock, while you changed my wages ten times. [42]If the God of my father, the God of Abraham and the Fear of Isaac, had not been on my side, you would now have sent me away empty-handed. But God saw my plight and the fruits of my toil, and last night he reproached you."

[43]Laban replied to Jacob: "The daughters are mine, their children are mine, and the flocks are mine; everything you see belongs to me. What can I do now for my own daughters and for the children they have borne? [44]Come, now, let us make a covenant, you and I; and it will be a treaty between you and me."

[45]Then Jacob took a stone and set it up as a sacred pillar. [46]Jacob said to his kinsmen, "Gather stones." So they got stones and made a mound; and they ate there at the mound. [47]Laban called it Jegar-sahadutha, but Jacob called it Galeed. [48]Laban said, "This mound will be a witness from now on between you

---

up his search for the idols. She also demonstrates that she is as capable of trickery as her husband and her father.

In the fourth stage, verses 36-42, Jacob takes the offensive, rehearsing all the injustices he has suffered at Laban's hands since his arrival at his home twenty years ago.

In the fifth stage, verses 43-54, Laban proposes that the two of them make an agreement. This will assure him that his family will be safe in Jacob's care, and that the two families will not interfere with each other but will live in peaceful coexistence. They formalize the agreement by erecting a stone pillar and then sharing a meal. This meal probably includes only the two men, as Jacob then invites his men to share the meal in verse 54, after he offers a sacrifice. Both men give a name to the place, each in his own native language, further highlighting the separation that is taking place between the two families. Laban invokes the God of Abraham and the God of Nahor, the ancestral deities of both families. Jacob invokes his father's name, offers a sacrifice, and invites his men to the sacrificial meal to finalize the treaty.

and me." That is why it was named Galeed—[49]and also Mizpah, for he said: "May the LORD keep watch between you and me when we are out of each other's sight. [50]If you mistreat my daughters, or take other wives besides my daughters, know that even though no one else is there, God will be a witness between you and me."

[51]Laban said further to Jacob: "Here is this mound, and here is the sacred pillar that I have set up between you and me. [52]This mound will be a witness, and this sacred pillar will be a witness, that, with hostile intent, I may not pass beyond this mound into your territory, nor may you pass beyond it into mine. [53]May the God of Abraham and the God of Nahor, the God of their father, judge between us!" Jacob took the oath by the Fear of his father Isaac. [54]He then offered a sacrifice on the mountain and invited

his kinsmen to share in the meal. When they had eaten, they passed the night on the mountain.

32 [1]Early the next morning, Laban kissed his grandchildren and his daughters and blessed them; then he set out on his journey back home. [2]Meanwhile Jacob continued on his own way, and God's angels encountered him. [3]When Jacob saw them he said, "This is God's encampment." So he named that place Mahanaim.

Envoys to Esau. [4]Jacob sent messengers ahead to his brother Esau in the land of Seir, the country of Edom, [5]ordering them: "Thus you shall say to my lord Esau: 'Thus says your servant Jacob: I have been residing with Laban and have been delayed until now. [6]I own oxen, donkeys and sheep, as well as male and female servants. I have sent my lord this message in the hope of gaining your

32:1-3 The final leave-taking

Both parties spend the night in proximity to each other, and then Laban bids his family farewell and the two parties separate. This final scene is stark in its simplicity after the many duplicitous actions throughout Jacob's stay with Laban. As Jacob begins his journey homeward, angels appear, just as they did when he first left his parents' home at the beginning of his journey to Haran (28:12). While they do not take an active part in events, they mark the stages of Jacob's journey and the presence of God with Jacob in his travels.

32:4–33:20 The meeting of Jacob and Esau

When Jacob sets out, his first project is to make contact with his brother Esau. Jacob fled from his parents' home after he usurped the blessing intended for Esau, and Esau vowed to kill him (27:41). Now he returns home with a large family, and must protect both them and himself from harm. His honor as head of his family and also his promise to Laban demand that he take whatever steps are necessary toward this end.

favor.'" [7]When the messengers returned to Jacob, they said, "We found your brother Esau. He is now coming to meet you, and four hundred men are with him."

[8]Jacob was very much frightened. In his anxiety, he divided the people who were with him, as well as his flocks, herds and camels, into two camps. [9]"If Esau should come and attack one camp," he reasoned, "the remaining camp may still escape." [10]Then Jacob prayed: "God of my father Abraham and God of my father Isaac! You, LORD, who said to me, 'Go back to your land and your relatives, and I will be good to you.' [11]I am unworthy of all the acts of kindness and faithfulness that you have performed for your servant: although I crossed the Jordan here with nothing but my staff, I have now grown into two camps. [12]Save me from the hand of my brother, from the hand of Esau! Otherwise I fear that he will come and strike me down and the mothers with the children. [13]You yourself said, 'I will be very good to you, and I will make your descendants like the sands of the sea, which are too numerous to count.'"

[14]After passing the night there, Jacob selected from what he had with him a present for his brother Esau: [15]two hundred she-goats and twenty he-goats; two hundred ewes and twenty rams; [16]thirty female camels and their young; forty cows and ten bulls; twenty female donkeys and ten male donkeys. [17]He put these animals in the care of his servants, in separate herds, and he told the servants, "Go on ahead of me, but keep some space between the herds." [18]He ordered the servant in the lead, "When my brother Esau meets you and asks, 'To whom do you belong? Where are you going? To whom do these animals ahead of you belong?' [19]tell him, 'To your servant Jacob, but they have been sent as a gift to my lord Esau. Jacob himself is

---

Verses 4-22 describe four steps he takes in preparation for meeting his brother. First, he sends messengers with a conciliatory word to Esau, who sends word in return that he and his army will meet Jacob. Next, fearing for the safety of himself and his family, he divides his party into two groups. That way, if harm comes to one, the other will be spared. Then he prays to the God of his ancestors for help, recalling the promises God made to him when he started out from home (28:13-15) and when he began his journey home from Haran (31:3). Fearing what his brother might do to him and his family, he reminds God of the divine promise of descendants. His prayer calls on God's faithfulness rather than any claim of his own to divine care. Finally, he selects an extravagant number of livestock to give to his brother, and sends them ahead in droves, each in the care of one of his servants. After making all these preparations, he sends his family across the Jabbok, and he stays behind for the night. Crossing the Jabbok marks the family's entry into Jacob's homeland.

right behind us.'" ²⁰He also ordered the second servant and the third and all the others who followed behind the herds: "Thus and so you shall say to Esau, when you reach him; ²¹and also tell him, 'Your servant Jacob is right behind us.'" For Jacob reasoned, "If I first appease him with a gift that precedes me, then later, when I face him, perhaps he will forgive me." ²²So the gifts went on ahead of him, while he stayed that night in the camp.

Jacob's New Name. ²³That night, however, Jacob arose, took his two wives, with the two maidservants and his eleven children, and crossed the ford of the Jabbok. ²⁴After he got them and brought them across the wadi and brought over what belonged to him, ²⁵Jacob was left there alone. Then a man wrestled with him until the break of dawn. ²⁶When the man saw that he could not prevail over him, he struck Jacob's hip at its socket, so that Jacob's socket was dislocated as he wrestled with him. ²⁷The man then said, "Let me go, for it is daybreak." But Jacob said, "I will not let you go until you bless me." ²⁸"What is your name?" the man asked. He answered, "Jacob." ²⁹Then the man said, "You shall no longer be named Jacob, but Israel, because you have contended with divine and human beings and have prevailed." ³⁰Jacob then asked him, "Please tell me your name." He answered, "Why do you ask for my name?" With that, he blessed him. ³¹Jacob named the place Peniel, "because I have seen God face to face," he said, "yet my life has been spared."

³²At sunrise, as he left Penuel, Jacob limped along because of his hip. ³³That

---

Verses 23-33 give a vague description of a curious incident: an unidentified man wrestles with Jacob until dawn. The narrative does not identify the person or give information about where he came from or how he happened to find Jacob until the end of the incident. When the stranger realizes he cannot defeat Jacob he injures his hip, leaving Jacob with a limp. Then the man asks to be released, suggesting that Jacob the heel-grabber has him in his grasp. Jacob agrees on condition that the man bless him. He gives Jacob the new name of Israel, but refuses to tell Jacob his own name, and then disappears as mysteriously as he came. The name Jacob gives to the place, Peniel, lets us know that his assailant is God. This mysterious episode describes a universal human experience of passing a restless night wrestling out a dilemma. By the time the sun rises Jacob has faced down the enemy and has come to a new awareness that God is with him. A brief etiological note follows, connecting Jacob's hip injury with the custom of not eating the sciatic nerve. Here for the first time the narrative uses the term "Israelites" in honor of Jacob's new name; it appears frequently throughout the Old Testament.

is why, to this day, the Israelites do not eat the sciatic muscle that is on the hip socket, because he had struck Jacob's hip socket at the sciatic muscle.

33 **Jacob and Esau Meet.** ¹Jacob looked up and saw Esau coming, and with him four hundred men. So he divided his children among Leah, Rachel, and the two maidservants, ²putting the maidservants and their children first, Leah and her children next, and Rachel and Joseph last. ³He himself went on ahead of them, bowing to the ground seven times, until he reached his brother. ⁴Esau ran to meet him, embraced him, and flinging himself on his neck, kissed him as he wept.

⁵Then Esau looked up and saw the women and children and asked, "Who are these with you?" Jacob answered, "They are the children with whom God has graciously favored your servant."

⁶Then the maidservants and their children came forward and bowed low; ⁷next, Leah and her children came forward and bowed low; lastly, Joseph and Rachel came forward and bowed low. ⁸Then Esau asked, "What did you intend with all those herds that I encountered?" Jacob answered, "It was to gain my lord's favor." ⁹Esau replied, "I have plenty; my brother, you should keep what is yours." ¹⁰"No, I beg you!" said Jacob. "If you will do me the favor, accept this gift from me, since to see your face is for me like seeing the face of God—and you have received me so kindly. ¹¹Accept the gift I have brought you. For God has been generous toward me, and I have an abundance." Since he urged him strongly, Esau accepted.

¹²Then Esau said, "Let us break camp and be on our way; I will travel in front of you." ¹³But Jacob replied: "As my lord

After all the preparations including Jacob's night of wrestling with the angel, the brothers meet in 33:1-20. The meeting is affectionate, respectful, yet guarded. When Jacob sees his brother coming with his four hundred men, he arranges his wives and their maids with their respective children, in order of importance and affection. Jacob's bow repeats Abraham's gesture when he received the three visitors in 18:2. It is also ironic in light of the divine words to Rebekah when the twins were still in the womb (25:23) and Isaac's blessing of Jacob in 27:29. Esau's tender, affectionate greeting reverses the kiss Isaac gave Jacob when Jacob stole Esau's blessing.

After their greeting the conversation becomes cautious when Esau inquires about all the gifts Jacob has brought. He demurs, perhaps according to custom, perhaps in an effort not to be beholden to his brother. Jacob remains respectful and deferential, and makes a connection between seeing Esau and encountering his assailant the previous night when he refers to the face of God. Esau accepts Jacob's gifts but does not offer any in return: Jacob's gifts are restitution for past wrongs rather than fraternal offerings.

knows, the children are too young. And the flocks and herds that are nursing are a concern to me; if overdriven for even a single day, the whole flock will die. [14]Let my lord, then, go before his servant, while I proceed more slowly at the pace of the livestock before me and at the pace of my children, until I join my lord in Seir." [15]Esau replied, "Let me at least put at your disposal some of the people who are with me." But Jacob said, "Why is this that I am treated so kindly, my lord?" [16]So on that day Esau went on his way back to Seir, [17]and Jacob broke camp for Succoth. There Jacob built a home for himself and made booths for his livestock. That is why the place was named Succoth.

[18]Jacob arrived safely at the city of Shechem, which is in the land of Canaan, when he came from Paddan-aram. He encamped in sight of the city. [19]The plot of ground on which he had pitched his tent he bought for a hundred pieces of money from the descendants of Hamor, the father of Shechem. [20]He set up an altar there and invoked "El, the God of Israel."

34 **The Rape of Dinah.** [1]Dinah, the daughter whom Leah had borne to Jacob, went out to visit some of the women of the land. [2]When Shechem, son of Hamor the Hivite, the leader of the region, saw her, he seized her and lay with her by force. [3]He was strongly attracted to Dinah, daughter of Jacob, and

---

The brothers arrange to continue their travels, negotiating whether to journey together or separately. The narrative suggests hesitancy on Jacob's part when he prefers to travel apart from Esau's men. In fact, Jacob does not follow Esau as he said he would, but goes in the opposite direction and establishes a temporary home for his family. The brothers leave each other on that somewhat wary note.

Jacob and his family stay temporarily at Succoth, then continue on to Shechem where the Lord appeared to Abraham when he first came into the land (12:6). There Jacob purchases land from the Shechemites and builds an altar to the God of Israel, his new name. This is the second purchase of land recorded in Genesis; the first is the burial place for Sarah. The narrative does not specify the purpose for which this purchase will be used; it seems to represent Jacob's belief that God will continue to care for him and his family in their new home. But the following chapters show that Jacob's hope of peaceful settlement in the land is mistaken.

34:1-31 Dinah among the Shechemites

The narrative then focuses on Dinah, who goes out to meet her new neighbors. By specifying that she is Leah's daughter the narrative casts her in a negative light. Her action has been interpreted in both positive and

was in love with the young woman. So he spoke affectionately to her. ⁴Shechem said to his father Hamor, "Get me this young woman for a wife."

⁵Meanwhile, Jacob heard that Shechem had defiled his daughter Dinah; but since his sons were out in the field with his livestock, Jacob kept quiet until they came home. ⁶Now Hamor, the father of Shechem, went out to discuss the matter with Jacob, ⁷just as Jacob's sons were coming in from the field. When they heard the news, the men were indignant and extremely angry. Shechem had committed an outrage in Israel by lying with Jacob's daughter; such a thing is not done. ⁸Hamor appealed to them, saying: "My son Shechem has his heart set on your daughter. Please give her to him as a wife. ⁹Intermarry with us; give your daughters to us, and take our daughters for yourselves. ¹⁰Thus you can live among us. The land is open before you. Settle and move about freely in it and acquire holdings here." ¹¹Then Shechem appealed to Dinah's father and brothers: "Do me this favor, and whatever you ask from me, I will give. ¹²No matter how high you set the bridal price and gift, I will give you whatever you ask from me; only give me the young woman as a wife."

Revenge of Jacob's Sons. ¹³Jacob's sons replied to Shechem and his father Hamor with guile, speaking as they did

negative ways: either she is innocently exploring her new neighborhood or looking for companionship, or she acts inappropriately in going among Canaanites or leaving the family compound (see 24:3, 37). Perhaps the ambiguity of the statement leaves open all the above possibilities. She goes out to see the women, and is seen by the son of the chief, Hamor. She goes out as an active young woman and immediately becomes a passive victim. Things happen quickly, as the rapid succession of verbs indicates. The actions that follow are equally startling because of the abrupt shift they express.

In verse 5 the scene shifts to Dinah's father Jacob, who hears about the incident but decides against taking any action because his sons are working in the fields. This is an odd stance for Jacob, who usually takes matters in hand and finds ways to deal with complicated situations. Jacob apparently sends for his sons, who arrive to find Shechem's father Hamor making his request to their father. The brothers react with indignation to what Shechem has done: he did not simply violate Dinah and her entire family, but violated the moral climate of the community.

Several aspects of the narrative are complicated by layers of editing within the text. From a legal perspective Dinah's family is entitled to the bride-price for a virgin, but because Jacob is a resident alien, his claim to restitution is unclear. The relevant law in Exodus 22:15-16 reflects a time

because he had defiled their sister Dinah. [14]They said to them, "We are not able to do this thing: to give our sister to an uncircumcised man. For that would be a disgrace for us. [15]Only on this condition will we agree to that: that you become like us by having every male among you circumcised. [16]Then we will give you our daughters and take your daughters in marriage; we will settle among you and become one people. [17]But if you do not listen to us and be circumcised, we will take our daughter and go."

[18]Their proposal pleased Hamor and his son Shechem. [19]The young man lost no time in acting on the proposal, since he wanted Jacob's daughter. Now he was more highly regarded than anyone else in his father's house. [20]So Hamor and his son Shechem went to the gate of their city and said to the men of their city: [21]"These men are friendly toward us. Let them settle in the land and move about in it freely; there is ample room in the land for them. We can take their daughters in marriage and give our daughters to them. [22]But only on this condition will the men agree to live with us and form one people with us: that every male among us be circumcised as they themselves are. [23]Would not their livestock, their property, and all their animals then

---

later than the ancestral period. In addition, the second half of verse 7 judges Shechem's sin in language typical of the monarchic period rather than the time of the ancestors.

In verse 8 Hamor ignores the moral question and focuses on the political and economic benefit to Jacob's family if Dinah is given to Shechem in marriage. Shechem then enters the conversation and offers to give whatever is appropriate, apparently acknowledging that his defilement of Dinah requires some sort of restitution.

Jacob's sons outwardly maintain their focus on the religious and ethical dimension of the situation; they object to their sister marrying an uncircumcised man. Only if all the Shechemite males agree to be circumcised can Dinah's brothers agree to the marriage. In fact, in making this assertion they show themselves as capable of deception as their father (v. 13). Their intent is not to observe the religious custom; it is rather to set a trap for the men of Shechem.

Hamor and Shechem agree immediately to the brothers' request. One wonders if they realize the implications of the request: do they see it as a religious act? a political bargain? a ruse? The narrative does not specify. We suspect they anticipate the economic gain because, when they urge the men of the city to comply, they add a detail that is unknown to Dinah's brothers: the people of Shechem will then possess the livestock that belong to Jacob's family. The men of the city readily agree to the procedure.

be ours? Let us just agree with them, so that they will settle among us."

²⁴All who went out of the gate of the city listened to Hamor and his son Shechem, and all the males, all those who went out of the gate of the city, were circumcised. ²⁵On the third day, while they were still in pain, two of Jacob's sons, Simeon and Levi, brothers of Dinah, each took his sword, advanced against the unsuspecting city and massacred all the males. ²⁶After they had killed Hamor and his son Shechem with the sword, they took Dinah from Shechem's house and left. ²⁷Then the other sons of Jacob followed up the slaughter and sacked the city because their sister had been defiled. ²⁸They took their sheep, cattle and donkeys, whatever was in the city and in the surrounding country. ²⁹They carried off all their wealth, their children, and their women, and looted whatever was in the houses.

³⁰Jacob said to Simeon and Levi: "You have brought trouble upon me by making me repugnant to the inhabitants of the land, the Canaanites and the Perizzites. I have so few men that, if these people unite against me and attack me, I and my household will be wiped out." ³¹But they retorted, "Should our sister be treated like a prostitute?"

The loyalty among Dinah and her full brothers is evident in their next move. While the men are recuperating from the procedure, and are in great pain, two of her full brothers (that is, the sons of Leah), Simeon and Levi, kill all the males including Hamor and Shechem, then take Dinah from Shechem's house. Again the text leaves us wondering: is this a forceful removal or a rescue? Is Dinah eager to leave or reluctant? The text does not specify. Then Jacob's other sons completely sack the city and take the spoils for themselves.

Jacob finally takes a stand in verse 30, chastising Simeon and Levi for destroying Shechem. (Jacob's deathbed curse of these two sons in 49:5-7 reflects his outraged response to this destruction.) His response is startling: Jacob reprimands the two sons who come to Dinah's rescue, after he seems to have chosen not to make an issue of the terrible violation to her and to the entire family. Now that he has purchased a piece of land in the area, he hopes to live there in peace with the neighboring people who greatly outnumber them. He thinks of the number of his men, small in comparison to his neighbors. The brothers think of avenging the outrage to their sister and their entire family. Their final question summarizes the ambivalence and lack of resolution between father and sons and between competing values as the family settles in the land. Family concerns must be weighed in relation to relations with neighbors, and there are no easy answers.

35 **Bethel Revisited.** ¹God said to Jacob: Go up now to Bethel. Settle there and build an altar there to the God who appeared to you when you were fleeing from your brother Esau. ²So Jacob told his household and all who were with him: "Get rid of the foreign gods among you; then purify yourselves and change your clothes. ³Let us now go up to Bethel so that I might build an altar there to the God who answered me in the day of my distress and who has been with me wherever I have gone." ⁴They gave Jacob all the foreign gods in their possession and also the rings they had in their ears and Jacob buried them under the oak that is near Shechem. ⁵Then, as they set out, a great terror fell upon the surrounding towns, so that no one pursued the sons of Jacob.

⁶Thus Jacob and all the people who were with him arrived in Luz (now Bethel) in the land of Canaan. ⁷There he built an altar and called the place El-Bethel, for it was there that God had revealed himself to him when he was fleeing from his brother. ⁸Deborah, Rebekah's nurse, died. She was buried under the oak below Bethel, and so it was named Allon-bacuth.

35:1-29 Jacob settles in the land

Chapter 35 includes several episodes that seem at first glance to be isolated incidents in Jacob's life. In actuality each one relates to the whole cycle of stories about Jacob, showing that his life has come full circle during his absence from his father's house. The conniving, energetic youth who fled from his brother Esau has become a cautious father and protector of his land. This part of the narrative appears to be a compilation of stories from different sources; as a result we find incidents that appear to duplicate previous episodes. The chapter includes Jacob's visit to Bethel, the birth of his and Rachel's son Benjamin and the death of Rachel, Reuben's violation of Rachel's maid Bilhah, and the death and burial of Isaac.

After the massacre of the Shechemites, Jacob leaves that area at God's command and goes to Bethel. Jacob's threefold instruction depicts the preparations for departure as a liturgical act: he instructs them to dispose of their idols, purify themselves, and change clothes. Jacob follows the route taken by Abraham from Haran to Shechem and then to Bethel (12:4-8). The episode alludes to Jacob's night at Bethel when he fled from his brother Esau after stealing the blessing from their father (28:10-22). This time Jacob and his entire family are fleeing from the neighbors of the Shechemites. During his first stay at Bethel God promised to be with him in all his travels; now the family returns to the site to build an altar in thanks to God for fulfilling that promise. The people obey Jacob's three commands, and they set out on

⁹On Jacob's arrival from Paddan-aram, God appeared to him again and blessed him. ¹⁰God said to him:

Your name is Jacob.
You will no longer be named Jacob,
but Israel will be your name.

So he was named Israel. ¹¹Then God said to him: I am God Almighty; be fruitful and multiply. A nation, indeed an assembly of nations, will stem from you, and kings will issue from your loins. ¹²The land I gave to Abraham and Isaac I will give to you; and to your descendants after you I will give the land.

¹³Then God departed from him. ¹⁴In the place where God had spoken with him, Jacob set up a sacred pillar, a stone pillar, and upon it he made a libation and poured out oil. ¹⁵Jacob named the place where God spoke to him Bethel.

Jacob's Family. ¹⁶Then they departed from Bethel; but while they still had some distance to go to Ephrath, Rachel went into labor and suffered great distress. ¹⁷When her labor was most intense, the midwife said to her, "Do not fear, for now you have another son." ¹⁸With her last breath—for she was at the point of death—she named him Ben-oni; but his

their journey of purification after the defilement of chapter 34. God continues to protect the travelers from the local people as they make their way to Bethel, where Jacob reiterates his earlier promise to honor God (28:19-22).

A very brief announcement of the death of Rebekah's nurse Deborah follows in verse 8, with the note that she is buried under a particular oak at Bethel. With her death Jacob's family relinquishes one of the few remaining ties with Laban and his land. Earlier they gave up another tie when Jacob buried their idols near Shechem (perhaps these were idols the family members brought with them from Haran, or perhaps they were part of the booty seized at Shechem).

In verse 9 the narrative relates another experience of Jacob at Bethel. God appears to him and gives him the name Israel; earlier the mysterious stranger gave him the name (32:29); here it comes directly from God. God also promises him descendants, a nation, and land in language similar to the promises to Abraham in 17:6-8, and to Jacob on his earlier visit (28:13-15). God specifies that these are the same promises given to his father and grandfather: now Jacob inherits them. Jacob sets up a stone pillar to mark the spot, blesses it, and names the place Bethel (see also 28:19). The similarities between this and earlier episodes suggest that they come from different sources; this version is associated with E.

Once again the family sets out and travels southward (v. 16). Rachel goes into very difficult labor and gives birth to a boy, thus bringing to fruition

father named him Benjamin. [19]Thus Rachel died; and she was buried on the road to Ephrath (now Bethlehem). [20]Jacob set up a sacred pillar on her grave, and the same pillar marks Rachel's grave to this day.

[21]Israel moved on and pitched his tent beyond Migdal-eder. [22]While Israel was encamped in that region, Reuben went and lay with Bilhah, his father's concubine. When Israel heard of it, he was greatly offended.

The sons of Jacob were now twelve. [23]The sons of Leah: Reuben, Jacob's first-born, Simeon, Levi, Judah, Issachar, and Zebulun; [24]the sons of Rachel: Joseph and Benjamin; [25]the sons of Rachel's maidservant Bilhah: Dan and Naphtali; [26]the sons of Leah's maidservant Zilpah: Gad and Asher. These are the sons of Jacob who were born to him in Paddan-aram.

[27]Jacob went home to his father Isaac at Mamre, in Kiriath-arba (now Hebron), where Abraham and Isaac had resided. [28]The length of Isaac's life was one hundred and eighty years; [29]then he breathed his last. He died as an old man and was

the name she gave Joseph when he was born: a prayer that the Lord would give her another son (30:24). Rachel's last act is to name her newborn son, characterizing him as the son of her distress. Jacob, however, gives him the name Benjamin ("Son of the Right Hand"). Rachel dies and is buried on the road to Bethlehem, where the narrator specifies that the monument Jacob set up still marks the spot. Today the site designated as Rachel's tomb remains a place of pilgrimage, especially for pregnant women.

That incident is followed by the very brief note that Reuben, Leah's first son, sleeps with Bilhah, Rachel's maid, and Jacob finds out about it. Other biblical stories point to taking the concubine of the conquered enemy as a symbol of taking the defeated kingdom (see 2 Sam 3:7-8; 12:7-8; and 1 Kgs 2:13-25). In this case there is no further comment about the incident until Jacob condemns the act in his final testament in 49:3-4. Reuben's act backfires; he loses the birthright to which he is entitled as Jacob's first son just as Jacob's older brother Esau had done. A brief genealogical note follows in verses 22b-26, listing Jacob's twelve sons according to their mothers. Dinah is not included in the list.

A second brief note observes that Jacob returns to his father Isaac at Mamre, the place where both Isaac and Abraham had lived. Then Isaac dies and his two sons bury him, just as Isaac and Ishmael buried their father Abraham. In both instances, despite all the tensions among the siblings, they honor their fathers in death. Isaac's role in life was to carry forward the divine promises; he lives to see them handed over to his son Jacob.

gathered to his people. After a full life, his sons Esau and Jacob buried him.

36 **Edomite Lists.** ¹These are the descendants of Esau (that is, Edom). ²Esau took his wives from among the Canaanite women: Adah, daughter of Elon the Hittite; Oholibamah, the daughter of Anah the son of Zibeon the Hivite; ³and Basemath, daughter of Ishmael and sister of Nebaioth. ⁴Adah bore Eliphaz to Esau; Basemath bore Reuel; ⁵and Oholibamah bore Jeush, Jalam and Korah. These are the sons of Esau who were born to him in the land of Canaan.

⁶Esau took his wives, his sons, his daughters, and all the members of his household, as well as his livestock, all his cattle, and all the property he had acquired in the land of Canaan, and went to the land of Seir, away from his brother Jacob. ⁷Their possessions had become too great for them to dwell together, and the land in which they were residing could not support them because of their livestock. ⁸So Esau settled in the highlands of Seir. (Esau is Edom.) ⁹These are the descendants of Esau, ancestor of the Edomites, in the highlands of Seir.

¹⁰These are the names of the sons of Esau: Eliphaz, son of Adah, wife of Esau, and Reuel, son of Basemath, wife of Esau. ¹¹The sons of Eliphaz were Teman, Omar, Zepho, Gatam, and Kenaz. ¹²Timna was a concubine of Eliphaz, the son of Esau, and she bore Amalek to Eliphaz. Those were the sons of Adah, the wife of Esau. ¹³These were the sons of Reuel: Nahath, Zerah, Shammah, and Mizzah. Those were the sons of Basemath, the wife of Esau. ¹⁴These were the sons of Esau's wife Oholibamah—the daughter of Anah, son of Zibeon—whom she bore to Esau: Jeush, Jalam, and Korah.

¹⁵These are the clans of the sons of Esau. The sons of Eliphaz, Esau's firstborn: the clans of Teman, Omar, Zepho, Kenaz, ¹⁶Korah, Gatam, and Amalek. These are the clans of Eliphaz in the land

36:1-43 Esau's descendants

A detailed genealogy of Esau's descendants follows, interspersed with two other lists, the indigenous tribes of Seir and the Edomite kings. The lists are complicated because some of the information is given elsewhere, with a few variations. Verses 1-8 give the names of Esau's three wives and their children and grandchildren. Here the wives' names are Adah, a Hittite; Oholibamah, a Hivite; and Basemath, daughter of Ishmael; these differ slightly from the names given in 26:34 and 28:9: Judith, Basemath, and Mahalath. Adah and Basemath (according to the list in chapter 36) both bear one son to Esau; Oholibamah bears three.

Verses 9-14 list the children born to each of Esau's wives in Seir, where they settle after Jacob returns home. Adah's son has six sons of whom one is born to a concubine, and Basemath's son has four sons. The list does not name the grandsons of Basemath. The names are repeated in verses

of Edom; they are the sons of Adah. [17]These are the sons of Reuel, son of Esau: the clans of Nahath, Zerah, Shammah, and Mizzah. These are the clans of Reuel in the land of Edom; they are the sons of Basemath, wife of Esau. [18]These were the sons of Oholibamah, wife of Esau: the clans of Jeush, Jalam, and Korah. These are the clans of Esau's wife Oholibamah, daughter of Anah. [19]These are the sons of Esau—that is, Edom— according to their clans.

[20]These are the sons of Seir the Horite, the inhabitants of the land: Lotan, Shobal, Zibeon, Anah, [21]Dishon, Ezer, and Dishan; those are the clans of the Horites, sons of Seir in the land of Edom. [22]The sons of Lotan were Hori and Hemam, and Lotan's sister was Timna. [23]These are the sons of Shobal: Alvan, Mahanath, Ebal, Shepho, and Onam. [24]These are the sons of Zibeon: Aiah and Anah. He is the Anah who found water in the desert while he was pasturing the donkeys of his father Zibeon. [25]These are the children of Anah: Dishon and Oholibamah, daughter of Anah. [26]These are the sons of Dishon: Hemdan, Eshban, Ithran, and Cheran. [27]These are the sons of Ezer: Bilhan, Zaavan, and Akan. [28]These are the sons of Dishan: Uz and Aran. [29]These are the clans of the Horites: the clans of Lotan, Shobal, Zibeon, Anah, [30]Dishon, Ezer, and Dishan; those are the clans of the Horites, clan by clan, in the land of Seir.

[31]These are the kings who reigned in the land of Edom before any king reigned over the Israelites. [32]Bela, son of Beor, became king in Edom; the name of his city was Dinhabah. [33]When Bela died, Jobab, son of Zerah, from Bozrah, succeeded him as king. [34]When Jobab died, Husham, from the land of the Temanites,

---

15-19 with the inclusion of one additional grandson to Adah's descendants. Amalek, the son of the concubine, is listed as a full son with his brothers.

Verses 20-30 list the descendants of Seir, who become seven clans. Then verses 31-39 name the eight kings of Edom who ruled before the establishment of the monarchy in Israel. Finally, verses 40-43 name the eleven Edomite clans. These lists, attributed to P, represent the fulfillment of Isaac's blessing to Esau in 27:39-40: Esau will live far away and will be a warrior rather than a farmer. They also fulfill the Lord's words to Rebekah when the twins were still in her womb (25:23) that the older would serve the younger: Esau's descendants eventually serve the descendants of Jacob.

The lists attest to the long history of the early inhabitants of the land, and illustrate the ongoing intermingling of the peoples throughout history. They also witness to the ongoing divine protection of the people throughout all their comings and goings in the region. After these genealogical notes the focus of the narrative shifts to Jacob's son Joseph, the first son of his beloved wife Rachel, who died giving birth to her second son Benjamin.

succeeded him as king. [35]When Husham died, Hadad, son of Bedad, succeeded him as king. He is the one who defeated Midian in the country of Moab; the name of his city was Avith. [36]When Hadad died, Samlah, from Masrekah, succeeded him as king. [37]When Samlah died, Shaul, from Rehoboth-on-the-River, succeeded him as king. [38]When Shaul died, Baal-hanan, son of Achbor, succeeded him as king. [39]When Baal-hanan, son of Achbor, died, Hadad succeeded him as king; the name of his city was Pau. His wife's name was Mehetabel, the daughter of Matred, son of Mezahab.

[40]These are the names of the clans of Esau identified according to their families and localities: the clans of Timna, Alvah, Jetheth, [41]Oholibamah, Elah, Pinon, [42]Kenaz, Teman, Mibzar, [43]Magdiel, and Iram. Those are the clans of the Edomites, according to their settlements in their territorial holdings—that is, of Esau, the ancestor of the Edomites.

THE ANCESTRAL STORY
PART 4: THE JOSEPH STORY

Genesis 37:1–50:26

Both the focus and the genre of the narrative shift at this point. While the ancestral story in chapters 12–36 consists of a series of anecdotes arranged in episodic order (that is, separate episodes, loosely connected to one another but not moving toward a climax), the Joseph story has a unified plot that reaches toward a climax. The narrative is called a novella, or short novel. The term implies that the story is fictional; in fact, just as we do not know the precise historicity of the previous chapters, neither do we know the exact historical details of the Joseph narrative. What we do know is that the ancient narrative recounts God's continuing care for the people as promised from the time of Noah to the people in general, and promised in particular to Abraham and his family. The story of Joseph relates that ongoing care for the people as they move to Egypt, setting the stage for the exodus to come.

We have seen that the sons of Leah have a penchant for getting into trouble. Here we learn that the sons of Jacob's beloved, deceased Rachel, and especially Joseph her firstborn, are their father's favorites. This favoritism exacerbates the relationships among the twelve brothers, creating the conditions for several complications, expressed in familiar themes that continue to weave their way through the narrative; for example, competition among the brothers, similar to that between wives and brothers in

37 **Joseph Sold into Egypt.** [1]Jacob settled in the land where his father had sojourned, the land of Canaan. [2]This is the story of the family of Jacob. When Joseph was seventeen years old, he was tending the flocks with his brothers; he was an assistant to the sons of his father's wives Bilhah and Zilpah, and Joseph brought their father bad reports about them. [3]Israel loved Joseph best of all his sons, for he was the child of his old age; and he had made him a long ornamented tunic. [4]When his brothers saw that their father loved him best of all his brothers, they hated him so much that they could not say a kind word to him.

[5]Once Joseph had a dream, and when he told his brothers, they hated him even more. [6]He said to them, "Listen to this dream I had. [7]There we were, binding sheaves in the field, when suddenly my sheaf rose to an upright position, and your sheaves formed a ring around my sheaf and bowed down to it." [8]His brothers said to him, "Are you really going to make yourself king over us? Will you rule over us?" So they hated him all the more because of his dreams and his reports.

previous generations; and younger versus older as was the case between Esau and Jacob, and between Ishmael and Isaac.

Articles of clothing figure prominently here. Likewise, dreams also play a prominent part in the story, as does the theme of divine promise in jeopardy, protected by God. The story also records reversals of various kinds: in geographic locations, weather conditions, relationships among the family members, the fortunes of different brothers, Jacob's hopes and fears, to name a few. A further characteristic of the story is the influence of the wisdom tradition, which emphasizes human wit. Divine intervention is indirect: there are no visions, but the narrative specifies at different points that God continues to direct the affairs of Joseph and his family.

37:1-36 The sale of Joseph into slavery

The story resumes where it left off at the end of chapter 35: Jacob and his family are settled in Hebron. The narrative now focuses on Joseph, a seventeen-year-old shepherd who works with his brothers. The narrative immediately introduces the tension among the brothers, reporting that Joseph tells his father tales on Bilhah's and Zilpah's sons, with whom he works as an assistant (he is younger than ten of his brothers and also his sister Dinah). We are not told whether his reports to his father are true or false, only that Joseph breaks ranks with his brothers by reporting on them. Then the cause of the tension is revealed: Joseph is his father's favorite, and his father singles him out for preferential treatment.

⁹Then he had another dream, and told it to his brothers. "Look, I had another dream," he said; "this time, the sun and the moon and eleven stars were bowing down to me." ¹⁰When he told it to his father and his brothers, his father reproved him and asked, "What is the meaning of this dream of yours? Can it be that I and your mother and your brothers are to come and bow to the ground before you?" ¹¹So his brothers were furious at him but his father kept the matter in mind.

¹²One day, when his brothers had gone to pasture their father's flocks at Shechem, ¹³Israel said to Joseph, "Are your brothers not tending our flocks at Shechem? Come and I will send you to them." "I am ready," Joseph answered. ¹⁴"Go then," he replied; "see if all is well with your brothers and the flocks, and bring back word." So he sent him off from the valley of Hebron. When Joseph reached Shechem, ¹⁵a man came upon him as he was wandering about in the fields. "What are you looking for?" the

Jacob gives Joseph a special garment. This item has been the subject of much discussion and illustration, including the title of the musical *Joseph and the Amazing Technicolor Dreamcoat.* The actual meaning of the Hebrew word is uncertain: translations include a long-sleeved garment, one with many colors or special ornamentation, and one that reaches to the floor. While the meaning is uncertain, the idea is clear: Joseph receives a special garment from his father who dotes on him, and this creates bitter envy and rivalry on the part of his brothers, to the point that they can barely speak to him.

Joseph has a talent for interpreting dreams, understood in the ancient world as a gift from God, since dreams were thought to be divine revelations. In the Joseph narrative the dreams are symbolic in contrast to the straightforward words from God in earlier chapters of Genesis. The dreams appear in pairs, with different symbols giving the same message. This duplication assures that the dreams are genuine, and that their message is clear.

Joseph's report of his dreams exacerbates the tension between his brothers and him for two reasons: first, because the fact of his having the dreams singles him out as the recipient of a special gift; and second, because of the subject of the dreams. Both the dream of the crops and that of the stars deliver the same message: his brothers will be subservient to him. Here the younger-older motif begins to factor into the story.

The second dream includes not only his brothers but also his parents among those who will be subservient to him. The mention of his mother

man asked him. [16]"I am looking for my brothers," he answered. "Please tell me where they are tending the flocks." [17]The man told him, "They have moved on from here; in fact, I heard them say, 'Let us go on to Dothan.'" So Joseph went after his brothers and found them in Dothan. [18]They saw him from a distance, and before he reached them, they plot-ted to kill him. [19]They said to one another: "Here comes that dreamer! [20]Come now, let us kill him and throw him into one of the cisterns here; we could say that a wild beast devoured him. We will see then what comes of his dreams."

[21]But when Reuben heard this, he tried to save him from their hands, saying: "We must not take his life." [22]Then

---

is puzzling here since she has already died (35:19). Even Jacob questions Joseph about the second dream, but he "kept the matter in mind" (37:11). Throughout his own life Jacob received significant revelations in dreams; he can appreciate the importance of his son's dreams.

In Jacob's case it was his mother Rebekah who arranged that Jacob would receive his father's blessing, thus depriving Esau of what was rightfully his and feeding the tension between the two brothers. Now Jacob himself feeds the tension between Joseph and his brothers by showing favoritism to him. Joseph's awkwardly privileged position comes, then, partly from his father's actions and partly from the dreams.

In verse 13 Jacob sends Joseph to his brothers, who are tending the flocks at Shechem. Joseph's response, "hinneni," recalls other willing responses on the part of the ancestors when they are asked to do some significant task. Here Jacob directs Joseph to find his brothers and bring back a report on them. Perhaps he is concerned about their safety after their disastrous destruction of Shechem in chapter 34. The brothers have continued to move along with the grazing flocks, so by the time Joseph finds them they are at a considerable distance from home. The distance gives the brothers the opportunity to devise a plot against him without likelihood of detection: they plan to kill him and throw him into a cistern. Such an end would deprive Joseph of a proper burial, and thus dishonor him and them; the brothers are blinded to this possibility by their hatred and envy of him.

Reuben, the firstborn son, objects to killing his brother and offers an alternative: that they simply throw him into the cistern and not kill him. The narrative adds that Reuben hopes to rescue Joseph and return him to Jacob. As firstborn, he made an unsuccessful bid for power in violating Bilhah (35:22); here he unsuccessfully attempts to use his position in a positive way. Joseph reaches his brothers, wearing the infamous garment, which

Reuben said, "Do not shed blood! Throw him into this cistern in the wilderness; but do not lay a hand on him." His purpose was to save him from their hands and restore him to his father.

²³So when Joseph came up to his brothers, they stripped him of his tunic, the long ornamented tunic he had on; ²⁴then they took him and threw him into the cistern. The cistern was empty; there was no water in it.

²⁵Then they sat down to eat. Looking up, they saw a caravan of Ishmaelites coming from Gilead, their camels laden with gum, balm, and resin to be taken down to Egypt. ²⁶Judah said to his brothers: "What is to be gained by killing our brother and concealing his blood? ²⁷Come,

his brothers take from him; they throw him into the empty cistern, then sit down to enjoy a meal, indifferent to Joseph's plight and to their own evil.

In verse 25 the unexpected arrival of Ishmaelites offers an alternative opportunity, and the brothers arrange to sell their brother. (Egypt had a slave trade at the time.) Ironically, they explain their own hesitation to kill him because he is their brother, but that does not stop them from selling him or from deceiving their father about what they have done to him. A further irony rests in the family relationship among the descendants of Abraham: the brothers sell Joseph to their own relatives. (Recall that Ishmael was the son of Abraham by Hagar, the Egyptian maidservant of Sarah.) The mention of Midianites in verse 28 is puzzling. It might be a detail from the E strand in a passage that is primarily a J and P story, or it might relate that Joseph is sold several times before the Ishmaelites purchase him. Twenty shekels is the price of a slave between the ages of five and twenty, according to both the Code of Hammurabi and Leviticus 27:5; the weight of the pieces of silver in this passage is not known, but is most likely comparable. The passage very likely predates Leviticus, with the detail about the price coming from a later P insertion.

Reuben is not with his brothers when they sell Joseph. Later, when Reuben returns to the cistern to retrieve him, he discovers that Joseph is gone. The text is ambiguous as to whether his brothers know about his plan to rescue Joseph. But his anguished question expresses his consternation when he realizes Joseph is gone.

In verse 31 the brothers determine a way to break the news of Joseph's disappearance to their father. They use the infamous garment and the blood of a kid, two items that Jacob used long ago when he deceived his own father into giving him the blessing intended for Esau. When Jacob receives the bloody garment, his three exclamations show his gradual realization

let us sell him to these Ishmaelites, instead of doing away with him ourselves. After all, he is our brother, our own flesh." His brothers agreed. [28]Midianite traders passed by, and they pulled Joseph up out of the cistern. They sold Joseph for twenty pieces of silver to the Ishmaelites, who took him to Egypt.

[29]When Reuben went back to the cistern and saw that Joseph was not in it, he tore his garments, [30]and returning to his brothers, he exclaimed: "The boy is gone! And I—where can I turn?" [31]They took Joseph's tunic, and after slaughtering a goat, dipped the tunic in its blood. [32]Then they sent someone to bring the long ornamented tunic to their father, with the message: "We found this. See whether it is your son's tunic or not."

[33]He recognized it and exclaimed: "My son's tunic! A wild beast has devoured him! Joseph has been torn to pieces!" [34]Then Jacob tore his garments, put sackcloth on his loins, and mourned his son many days. [35]Though his sons and daughters tried to console him, he refused all consolation, saying, "No, I will go down mourning to my son in Sheol." Thus did his father weep for him.

[36]The Midianites, meanwhile, sold Joseph in Egypt to Potiphar, an official of Pharaoh and his chief steward.

38 **Judah and Tamar.** [1]About that time Judah went down, away from his brothers, and pitched his tent near a certain Adullamite named Hirah. [2]There Judah saw the daughter of a Canaanite named Shua; he married her,

of what it means: his beloved son Joseph is dead (37:33). Joseph's robe is the sign of his apparent death; Jacob's torn clothes are the sign of his grief. (Tearing one's garment was the customary sign of mourning.) Sheol, where Jacob expects to go after death, was the place deep under the earth where the spirits of all the deceased were believed to rest forever. It was not a place of reward or punishment.

Here the reader knows that Joseph is still alive. Jacob assumes his son is dead, and it is not clear what Joseph's brothers know about him. Meanwhile, the Midianites sell him into slavery to Potiphar, a courtier in the court of Pharaoh. This development jeopardizes the longstanding promise of descendants to Abraham, Isaac, and Jacob: Joseph is clearly his father's favorite and the one on whom we assume the promise rests; now he is a slave in Egypt.

38:1-30 Judah and Tamar

On the surface chapter 38 appears to be a digression from the Joseph narrative, but a closer look shows its connection. The narrative is vague about the chronology, stating simply, "About that time." Judah, who encouraged his brothers to sell Joseph rather than kill him, leaves his brothers and settles near Hirah the Adullamite. He marries a Canaanite woman and

and had intercourse with her. ³She conceived and bore a son, whom she named Er. ⁴Again she conceived and bore a son, whom she named Onan. ⁵Then she bore still another son, whom she named Shelah. She was in Chezib when she bore him.

⁶Judah got a wife named Tamar for his firstborn, Er. ⁷But Er, Judah's firstborn, greatly offended the LORD; so the LORD took his life. ⁸Then Judah said to Onan, "Have intercourse with your brother's wife, in fulfillment of your duty as brother-in-law, and thus preserve your brother's line." ⁹Onan, however, knew that the offspring would not be his; so whenever he had intercourse with his brother's wife, he wasted his seed on the ground, to avoid giving off-

spring to his brother. ¹⁰What he did greatly offended the LORD, and the LORD took his life too. ¹¹Then Judah said to his daughter-in-law Tamar, "Remain a widow in your father's house until my son Shelah grows up"—for he feared that Shelah also might die like his brothers. So Tamar went to live in her father's house.

¹²Time passed, and the daughter of Shua, Judah's wife, died. After Judah completed the period of mourning, he went up to Timnah, to those who were shearing his sheep, in company with his friend Hirah the Adullamite. ¹³Then Tamar was told, "Your father-in-law is on his way up to Timnah to shear his sheep." ¹⁴So she took off her widow's garments, covered herself with a shawl,

---

they have three sons. There is no stigma attached to marrying a Canaanite woman, unlike the situations for Isaac and Jacob (24:3; 28:6). Judah makes the customary arrangements for the marriage of his firstborn son Er to Tamar. Er sins (we are not told what his sin was) and the Lord takes his life in punishment. In keeping with the custom, Judah instructs his second son Onan to marry Tamar. Onan refuses to cooperate, interrupting intercourse and thus avoiding the conception of a child with Tamar. It is not clear whether he refuses to honor his deceased brother's name or whether he does not want to share his inheritance with a son. Whatever the reason, his negligence with regard to Tamar is a sin of disobedience for which the Lord takes Onan's life, leaving Judah with only one living son. At the time the levirate duty of a father-in-law to give his next son to the widow was obligatory; later law provided for the son to refuse this duty (Deut 25:5-9).

Judah does not wish to lose his only living son (v. 11), so he puts Tamar in an impossible position: he sends her back to her father's house, but does not release her from his family. Consequently she does not really belong to her father's family, but neither is she under the protection of Judah.

Years later Tamar takes an opportunity to force Judah's responsibility toward her (v. 12). She dresses like a prostitute (again clothing factors into the story) and places herself where he will see her as he travels to shear his

and having wrapped herself sat down at the entrance to Enaim, which is on the way to Timnah; for she was aware that, although Shelah was now grown up, she had not been given to him in marriage. [15]When Judah saw her, he thought she was a harlot, since she had covered her face. [16]So he went over to her at the roadside and said, "Come, let me have intercourse with you," for he did not realize that she was his daughter-in-law. She replied, "What will you pay me for letting you have intercourse with me?" [17]He answered, "I will send you a young goat from the flock." "Very well," she said, "provided you leave me a pledge until you send it." [18]Judah asked, "What pledge should I leave you?" She answered, "Your seal and cord, and the staff in your hand." So he gave them to her and had intercourse with her, and she conceived by him. [19]After she got up and went away, she took off her shawl and put on her widow's garments again.

[20]Judah sent the young goat by his friend the Adullamite to recover the pledge from the woman; but he did not find her. [21]So he asked the men of that place, "Where is the prostitute, the one

sheep. The text is careful not to judge him harshly: he does not recognize her because of her veil, and he had not planned to engage a prostitute, as he has nothing with which to pay her. (The usual fee was a kid.) Instead, she requests three items that can positively identify him: his seal, cord, and staff. Cylinder seals with a hole through the middle, through which a cord was run to hang the seals around the neck of their owners, were a means of marking documents: the seal was rolled in soft clay. When the clay hardened the mark of the seal remained, identifying the sender of the document and assuring that it had not been tampered with. The staff or walking stick probably had some particular mark of identification on it.

Tamar conceives a child, and returns to her widow's life. Judah, true to his word, sends his friend Hirah to deliver the promised goat to Tamar (v. 20). Just as a kid played a role in notifying Jacob that Joseph was thought to be dead, likewise a kid plays a role here in maintaining Judah's anonymity. Hirah inquires about the whereabouts of a cult prostitute, but there is no cult prostitute in the town. (Tamar posed as a prostitute, not a cult prostitute. The Hebrew words mark this distinction.) Hirah reports to Judah that he is unable to locate the woman, and Judah prefers to let the matter go rather than risk embarrassment.

In verse 24 Judah learns that Tamar is pregnant, but has no idea that he is the child's father. Acting on his authority as head of the family, he orders that she be burned, an exceptionally harsh means of death. But

by the roadside in Enaim?" But they answered, "No prostitute has been here." [22]He went back to Judah and told him, "I did not find her; and besides, the men of the place said, 'No prostitute has been here.'" [23]"Let her keep the things," Judah replied; "otherwise we will become a laughingstock. After all, I did send her this young goat, but you did not find her."

[24]About three months later, Judah was told, "Your daughter-in-law Tamar has acted like a harlot and now she is pregnant from her harlotry." Judah said, "Bring her out; let her be burned." [25]But as she was being brought out, she sent word to her father-in-law, "It is by the man to whom these things belong that I am pregnant." Then she said, "See whose seal and cord and staff these are." [26]Judah recognized them and said, "She is in the right rather than I, since I did not give her to my son Shelah." He had no further sexual relations with her.

[27]When the time of her delivery came, there were twins in her womb. [28]While she was giving birth, one put out his hand; and the midwife took and tied a

---

Tamar produces the three items to identify the father of her child, and Judah realizes what he has done. Tamar's words to Judah resemble those of the messenger who delivers Joseph's garment to Jacob in 37:32. Judah acknowledges his sin: he did not give his third son to Tamar, as the ancient custom required. He uses his prerogative as her father-in-law to condemn her, but he neglected to use it earlier when he refused to give his third son to her. Again the text is careful not to condemn him harshly: it specifies that he does not have intercourse with her again. The narrative also exonerates Tamar: Judah says about her, "She is in the right rather than I" (38:26). In fact, Judah placed Tamar in an impossible position by not giving his third son Shelah to her but at the same time not relieving her of any obligation to him as her father-in-law. Tamar does what is necessary to provide a son for her deceased husband and still remain faithful to her obligations as Judah's daughter-in-law.

Tamar gives birth to twins in verse 27. The red thread tied around the first hand to come out of the womb recalls the birth of Rebekah's twins: Esau, whose name means "red," was born first but was not the favored son (25:25-26). Zerah is Tamar's firstborn, but Perez, the second, is the favored one; we learn in Ruth 4:18-22 that he is the ancestor of David.

The chapter began by depicting Leah's fourth son in trouble, like her first three. But it ends with indications that he assumes responsibility for his actions. The next time we meet Judah is in 43:3, when he and his brothers are back at home with their father.

crimson thread on his hand, noting, "This one came out first." [29]But as he withdrew his hand, his brother came out; and she said, "What a breach you have made for yourself!" So he was called Perez. [30]Afterward his brother, who had the crimson thread on his hand, came out; he was called Zerah.

39 **Joseph's Temptation.** [1]When Joseph was taken down to Egypt, an Egyptian, Potiphar, an official of Pharaoh and his chief steward, bought him from the Ishmaelites who had brought him there. [2]The LORD was with Joseph and he enjoyed great success and was assigned to the household of his Egyptian master. [3]When his master saw that the LORD was with him and brought him success in whatever he did, [4]he favored Joseph and made him his personal attendant; he put him in charge of his household and entrusted to him all his possessions. [5]From the moment that he put him in charge of his household and all his possessions, the LORD blessed the Egyptian's house for Joseph's sake; the LORD's blessing was on everything he owned, both inside the house and out. [6]Having left everything he owned in Joseph's charge, he gave no thought, with Joseph there, to anything but the food he ate.

39:1-23 Joseph in the household of Potiphar

The Joseph story resumes where it left off in 37:36, with Joseph in the household of Potiphar, his new owner. For the first time in the Joseph story we read that the Lord is with Joseph. Throughout the Joseph story the Lord guides and protects Joseph, but the narrative seldom mentions him. In this chapter, however, the word "Lord" appears six times. Its only other appearance in the Joseph story is in Jacob's testament in 49:18. The word "God" appears much more frequently in the Joseph story.

Here another of Jacob's sons faces a critical situation with a woman. (Jacob himself had his own difficulties over women: he was given Leah, after being promised Rachel for a wife in 29:14-30.) Joseph fares well under Potiphar, thanks to divine protection and guidance. Furthermore, he is handsome, an additional sign of divine favor. His master leaves all the household responsibilities to Joseph. The description of Potiphar being attentive only to the food he eats suggests that he neglects his wife. The juxtaposition of contrasting descriptions of Potiphar and Joseph foreshadows trouble in his household, and it is not long in coming.

Potiphar's wife's speaks as a slave owner to a slave in her efforts to seduce him (v. 7). Joseph attributes his refusal to his faithfulness both to Potiphar and to God. But she refuses to give up, and finds a way when the two are alone. Once again Joseph's garment is a source of trouble for him.

119

Now Joseph was well-built and handsome. [7]After a time, his master's wife looked at him with longing and said, "Lie with me." [8]But he refused and said to his master's wife, "Look, as long as I am here, my master does not give a thought to anything in the house, but has entrusted to me all he owns. [9]He has no more authority in this house than I do. He has withheld from me nothing but you, since you are his wife. How, then, could I do this great wrong and sin against God?" [10]Although she spoke to him day after day, he would not agree to lie with her, or even be near her.

[11]One such day, when Joseph came into the house to do his work, and none of the household servants were then in the house, [12]she laid hold of him by his cloak, saying, "Lie with me!" But leaving the cloak in her hand, he escaped and ran outside. [13]When she saw that he had left his cloak in her hand as he escaped outside, [14]she cried out to her household servants and told them, "Look! My husband has brought us a Hebrew man to mock us! He came in here to lie with me, but I cried out loudly. [15]When he heard me scream, he left his cloak beside me and escaped and ran outside."

[16]She kept the cloak with her until his master came home. [17]Then she told him the same story: "The Hebrew slave whom you brought us came to me to amuse himself at my expense. [18]But when I screamed, he left his cloak beside me and escaped outside." [19]When the master heard his wife's story in which she reported, "Thus and so your servant did to me," he became enraged. [20]Joseph's master seized him and put him into the jail where the king's prisoners were confined. And there he sat, in jail.

[21]But the Lord was with Joseph, and showed him kindness by making the chief jailer well-disposed toward him.

She takes it to use against him by blackmailing him, just as his brothers did earlier when they took the garment his father gave him, and used it to insinuate that Joseph was dead. Tamar, on the other hand, took Judah's seal, cord, and staff for a different purpose. She held them in pledge until he would pay his debt to her, and eventually used them to identify him as the father of her children, saving her own life in the process.

Potiphar's wife is vengeful in her rejection and embarrassment, and she immediately accuses her husband of neglect in bringing a foreigner into the household. She claims to have screamed as evidence of her innocence; eventually the law required such an act if one was raped in a public place (Deut 22:23-27). Potiphar's lack of involvement continues, and he condemns Joseph, to whom he has entrusted his entire household, without even asking for his side of the story. Joseph is imprisoned in the royal prison, but the Lord is with him. The chief jailer puts Joseph in charge of the prison, just as Potiphar put him in charge of his household, and trusts him implicitly.

²²The chief jailer put Joseph in charge of all the prisoners in the jail. Everything that had to be done there, he was the one to do it. ²³The chief jailer did not have to look after anything that was in Joseph's charge, since the LORD was with him and was bringing success to whatever he was doing.

40 **The Dreams Interpreted.** ¹Some time afterward, the royal cupbearer and baker offended their lord, the king of Egypt. ²Pharaoh was angry with his two officials, the chief cupbearer and the chief baker, ³and he put them in custody in the house of the chief steward, the same jail where Joseph was confined. ⁴The chief steward assigned Joseph to them, and he became their attendant.

After they had been in custody for some time, ⁵the cupbearer and the baker of the king of Egypt who were confined in the jail both had dreams on the same night, each his own dream and each dream with its own meaning. ⁶When Joseph came to them in the morning, he saw that they looked disturbed. ⁷So he asked Pharaoh's officials who were with him in custody in his master's house, "Why do you look so troubled today?" ⁸They answered him, "We have had dreams, but there is no one to interpret them." Joseph said to them, "Do interpretations not come from God? Please tell me the dreams."

⁹Then the chief cupbearer told Joseph his dream. "In my dream," he said, "I saw a vine in front of me, ¹⁰and on the vine were three branches. It had barely budded when its blossoms came out, and its clusters ripened into grapes.

40:1-23 Joseph in prison

Eventually Pharaoh has two royal officials incarcerated in the same prison as Joseph. His gift for interpreting dreams serves him well when both officials have troubling dreams in the same night. Joseph offers to interpret the dreams, acknowledging that his ability comes from God. This statement dissociates his ability from that of the magicians in Pharaoh's court, whose duties include interpreting dreams. Both dreams involve the number three, a number that signifies completion. Here the number represents the number of days until the dreams come to pass. Numerology was often associated with wisdom in the ancient world. Joseph's ability to interpret numbers demonstrates that he has the divine gift of wisdom.

The cupbearer's dream, which he repeats in verses 9-11, relates to his duty in the court: as cupbearer he holds the cup from which the Pharaoh drinks. His character must be above reproach because it is his responsibility to be sure no one poisons the Pharaoh. Joseph interprets the dream, announcing to the cupbearer that he will soon be released from prison. Joseph asks in return that the cupbearer arrange for his release as soon as it is possible.

[11]Pharaoh's cup was in my hand; so I took the grapes, pressed them out into his cup, and put it in Pharaoh's hand." [12]Joseph said to him: "This is its interpretation. The three branches are three days; [13]within three days Pharaoh will single you out and restore you to your post. You will be handing Pharaoh his cup as you formerly did when you were his cupbearer. [14]Only think of me when all is well with you, and please do me the great favor of mentioning me to Pharaoh, to get me out of this place. [15]The truth is that I was kidnapped from the land of the Hebrews, and I have not done anything here that they should have put me into a dungeon."

[16]When the chief baker saw that Joseph had given a favorable interpretation, he said to him: "I too had a dream. In it I had three bread baskets on my head; [17]in the top one were all kinds of bakery products for Pharaoh, but the birds were eating them out of the basket on my head." [18]Joseph said to him in reply: "This is its interpretation. The three baskets are three days; [19]within three days Pharaoh will single you out and will impale you on a stake, and the birds will be eating your flesh."

[20]And so on the third day, which was Pharaoh's birthday, when he gave a banquet to all his servants, he singled out the chief cupbearer and chief baker in the midst of his servants. [21]He restored the chief cupbearer to his office, so that he again handed the cup to Pharaoh; [22]but the chief baker he impaled—just as Joseph had told them in his interpretation. [23]Yet the chief cupbearer did not think of Joseph; he forgot him.

41 **Pharaoh's Dream.** [1]After a lapse of two years, Pharaoh had a dream. He was standing by the Nile, [2]when up out of the Nile came seven cows, fine-looking and fat; they grazed

Then the baker repeats his own dream that, like the cupbearer's, relates to his office. This time Joseph's interpretation foreshadows an unfortunate outcome. In three days, the time designated in both dreams, both of Joseph's interpretations prove to be accurate: the cupbearer is restored to his office and the baker is impaled during a birthday banquet in Pharaoh's honor. The cupbearer does not remember Joseph, but completely forgets about him. His forgetting foreshadows the eventual experience of Jacob's descendants in Egypt when "a new king, who knew nothing of Joseph, rose to power" (Exod 1:8).

41:1-56 The exoneration of Joseph

Joseph's gift of interpreting dreams continues to serve him well. This time it is Pharaoh who has a troubling dream. It includes several ominous elements: the Nile, on which all the people depend for subsistence, and also cows that figure prominently in the economy of the people. It involves the

in the reed grass. ³Behind them seven other cows, poor-looking and gaunt, came up out of the Nile; and standing on the bank of the Nile beside the others, ⁴the poor-looking, gaunt cows devoured the seven fine-looking, fat cows. Then Pharaoh woke up.

⁵He fell asleep again and had another dream. He saw seven ears of grain, fat and healthy, growing on a single stalk. ⁶Behind them sprouted seven ears of grain, thin and scorched by the east wind; ⁷and the thin ears swallowed up the seven fat, healthy ears. Then Pharaoh woke up—it was a dream!

⁸Next morning his mind was agitated. So Pharaoh had all the magicians and sages of Egypt summoned and recounted his dream to them; but there was no one to interpret it for him. ⁹Then the chief cupbearer said to Pharaoh: "Now I remember my negligence! ¹⁰Once, when Pharaoh was angry with his servants, he put me and the chief baker in custody in the house of the chief steward. ¹¹Later, we both had dreams on the same night, and each of our dreams had its own meaning. ¹²There was a Hebrew youth with us, a slave of the chief steward; and when we told him our dreams, he interpreted them for us and explained for each of us the meaning of his dream. ¹³Things turned out just as he had told us: I was restored to my post, but the other man was impaled."

¹⁴Pharaoh therefore had Joseph summoned, and they hurriedly brought him from the dungeon. After he shaved and changed his clothes, he came to Pharaoh. ¹⁵Pharaoh then said to Joseph: "I had a dream but there was no one to interpret it. But I hear it said of you, 'If he hears a dream he can interpret it.'" ¹⁶"It is not I," Joseph replied to Pharaoh, "but God who will respond for the well-being of Pharaoh."

¹⁷Then Pharaoh said to Joseph: "In my dream, I was standing on the bank of the Nile, ¹⁸when up from the Nile came seven cows, fat and well-formed; they grazed in the reed grass. ¹⁹Behind them came seven other cows, scrawny,

number seven, a number that denotes completion. Furthermore, it shows the seven unhealthy cows eating the healthy ones. Then, as with Joseph's earlier dream, a second one follows, verifying the message of the first. This one also involves a subsistence item, corn, the number seven, and the unhealthy consuming the healthy. Pharaoh calls on his magicians to interpret the dream. When they fail to do so, the cupbearer finally remembers Joseph.

Verse 14 expresses the urgency of the situation in the rapid succession of preparatory actions. When Pharaoh explains his need to Joseph, Joseph is quick to point out that it is God, not himself, who interprets dreams. He repeats this three more times in his conversation with Pharaoh. Pharaoh reports the dreams to Joseph, adding details that highlight his anxiety. For

most ill-formed and gaunt. Never have I seen such bad specimens as these in all the land of Egypt! [20]The gaunt, bad cows devoured the first seven fat cows. [21]But when they had consumed them, no one could tell that they had done so, because they looked as bad as before. Then I woke up. [22]In another dream I saw seven ears of grain, full and healthy, growing on a single stalk. [23]Behind them sprouted seven ears of grain, shriveled and thin and scorched by the east wind; [24]and the seven thin ears swallowed up the seven healthy ears. I have spoken to the magicians, but there is no one to explain it to me."

[25]Joseph said to Pharaoh: "Pharaoh's dreams have the same meaning. God has made known to Pharaoh what he is about to do. [26]The seven healthy cows are seven years, and the seven healthy ears are seven years—the same in each dream. [27]The seven thin, bad cows that came up after them are seven years, as are the seven thin ears scorched by the east wind; they are seven years of fam-ine. [28]Things are just as I told Pharaoh: God has revealed to Pharaoh what he is about to do. [29]Seven years of great abundance are now coming throughout the land of Egypt; [30]but seven years of famine will rise up after them, when all the abundance will be forgotten in the land of Egypt. When the famine has exhausted the land, [31]no trace of the abundance will be found in the land because of the famine that follows it, for it will be very severe. [32]That Pharaoh had the same dream twice means that the matter has been confirmed by God and that God will soon bring it about.

[33]"Therefore, let Pharaoh seek out a discerning and wise man and put him in charge of the land of Egypt. [34]Let Pharaoh act and appoint overseers for the land to organize it during the seven years of abundance. [35]They should collect all the food of these coming good years, gathering the grain under Pharaoh's authority, for food in the cities, and they should guard it. [36]This food will serve as a reserve for the country

---

instance, he says about the cows, "Never have I seen such bad specimens as these in all the land of Egypt!" (41:19).

Joseph immediately explains to Pharaoh that the dreams are a revelation from God about what the next fourteen years will bring: seven years of plenty, followed by seven years of severe famine. Joseph offers a plan to prepare for the coming famine by stockpiling the surplus during the seven years of plenty to tide the people over during the impending years of famine. Pharaoh is so impressed with Joseph's wise advice that he makes him second in command only to himself, hoping that God will care for Egypt through Joseph (vv. 37-41). There is an implicit statement of faith in God here: Pharaoh relies on the God of Israel rather than on the Egyptian deities to see them through the imminent crisis.

against the seven years of famine that will occur in the land of Egypt, so that the land may not perish in the famine."

[37]This advice pleased Pharaoh and all his servants. [38]"Could we find another like him," Pharaoh asked his servants, "a man so endowed with the spirit of God?" [39]So Pharaoh said to Joseph: "Since God has made all this known to you, there is no one as discerning and wise as you are. [40]You shall be in charge of my household, and all my people will obey your command. Only in respect to the throne will I outrank you." [41]Then Pharaoh said to Joseph, "Look, I put you in charge of the whole land of Egypt." [42]With that, Pharaoh took off his signet ring and put it on Joseph's finger. He dressed him in robes of fine linen and put a gold chain around his neck. [43]He then had him ride in his second chariot, and they shouted "Abrek!" before him.

Thus was Joseph installed over the whole land of Egypt. [44]"I am Pharaoh," he told Joseph, "but without your approval no one shall lift hand or foot in all the land of Egypt." [45]Pharaoh also bestowed the name of Zaphenath-paneah on Joseph, and he gave him in marriage Asenath, the daughter of Potiphera, priest of Heliopolis. And Joseph went out over the land of Egypt. [46]Joseph was thirty years old when he entered the service of Pharaoh, king of Egypt.

After Joseph left Pharaoh, he went throughout the land of Egypt. [47]During the seven years of plenty, when the land produced abundant crops, [48]he collected all the food of these years of plenty that the land of Egypt was enjoying and stored it in the cities, placing in each city the crops of the fields around it. [49]Joseph collected grain like the sands of the sea, so much that at last he stopped measuring it, for it was beyond measure.

[50]Before the famine years set in, Joseph became the father of two sons, borne to him by Asenath, daughter of Potiphera, priest of Heliopolis. [51]Joseph named his firstborn Manasseh, meaning, "God has made me forget entirely my

An installation ceremony follows, beginning in verse 42. Once again clothes factor into the story when Pharaoh clothes Joseph in the trappings of rank: signet ring, linen robes, and chain around his neck. The three items are a flashback to the Tamar story: seal, cord, and staff were Judah's identification; here seal, chain, and linen robe are Pharaoh's signs of office. Then he is given a public ride in a royal chariot, probably horse-drawn. This is the first mention of the vehicle in the Bible. The meaning of the salute, "Abrek!" is not known; it is similar to an Egyptian word that means "Attention!" Joseph's new name is Egyptian, and has been interpreted several ways that relate to his gift for interpreting dreams or his new position in Pharaoh's court. His marriage makes him a member of a noble family (41:45). Joseph implements his plan of storing food during the time of plenty so it will be available for the time of famine. The surplus is huge beyond measure.

troubles and my father's house"; [52]and the second he named Ephraim, meaning, "God has made me fruitful in the land of my affliction."

[53]When the seven years of abundance enjoyed by the land of Egypt came to an end, [54]the seven years of famine set in, just as Joseph had said. Although there was famine in all the other countries, food was available throughout the land of Egypt. [55]When all the land of Egypt became hungry and the people cried to Pharaoh for food, Pharaoh said to all the Egyptians: "Go to Joseph and do whatever he tells you." [56]When the famine had spread throughout the land, Joseph opened all the cities that had grain and rationed it to the Egyptians, since the famine had gripped the land of Egypt. [57]Indeed, the whole world came to Egypt to Joseph to buy grain, for famine had gripped the whole world.

42 The Brothers' First Journey to Egypt.

[1]When Jacob learned that grain rations were for sale in Egypt, he said to his sons: "Why do you keep looking at one another?" [2]He went on, "I hear that grain is for sale in Egypt. Go down there and buy some for us, that we may stay alive and not die." [3]So ten of Joseph's brothers went down to buy grain from Egypt. [4]But Jacob did not send Joseph's brother Benjamin with his brothers, for he thought some disaster might befall him. [5]And so the sons of Israel were among those who came to buy grain, since there was famine in the land of Canaan.

[6]Joseph, as governor of the country, was the one who sold grain to all the people of the land. When Joseph's brothers came, they bowed down to him with their faces to the ground. [7]He recognized them as soon as he saw them. But he

During the time of prosperity Joseph fathers two sons, Manasseh and Ephraim (vv. 50-52), whose names relate to Joseph's past difficulties and present circumstances. Then the famine comes as predicted, and Pharaoh relies on Joseph to distribute the surplus grain so that everyone has plenty to eat. Eventually people come to Egypt from all over the world, seeking relief from the famine. This development sets the stage for Joseph's brothers to come to Egypt and be reunited with their brother.

42:1-38 The brothers' first journey to Egypt

Jacob and his family feel the effects of the famine, suffering from hunger and also from inability to find a solution for their desperate situation. It is Jacob who suggests a way out of their difficulty: he sends them to Egypt for rations. Ironically, he is sending them to their brother Joseph, just as he sent Joseph to his brothers long ago, precipitating his sale into slavery. He has resumed his place at the head of his family, after suffering the heartbreaking loss of his son Joseph. In fact, on account of losing Joseph he does not permit Benjamin to go with his brothers to Egypt because he does not want

concealed his own identity from them and spoke harshly to them. "Where do you come from?" he asked them. They answered, "From the land of Canaan, to buy food."

⁸When Joseph recognized his brothers, although they did not recognize him, ⁹he was reminded of the dreams he had about them. He said to them: "You are spies. You have come to see the weak points of the land." ¹⁰"No, my lord," they replied. "On the contrary, your servants have come to buy food. ¹¹All of us are sons of the same man. We are honest men; your servants have never been spies." ¹²But he answered them: "Not so! It is the weak points of the land that you have come to see." ¹³"We your servants," they said, "are twelve brothers, sons of a certain man in Canaan; but the youngest one is at present with our father, and the other one is no more." ¹⁴"It is just as I said," Joseph persisted; "you are spies. ¹⁵This is how you shall be tested: I swear by the life of Pharaoh that you shall not leave here unless your youngest brother comes here. ¹⁶So send one of your number to get your brother, while the rest of you stay here under arrest. Thus will your words be tested for their truth; if they are untrue, as Pharaoh lives, you are spies!" ¹⁷With that, he locked them up in the guardhouse for three days.

¹⁸On the third day Joseph said to them: "Do this, and you shall live; for I am a God-fearing man. ¹⁹If you are honest men, let one of your brothers be confined in this prison, while the rest of you go and take home grain for your starving families. ²⁰But you must bring me your youngest brother. Your words will thus be verified, and you will not die." To this they agreed. ²¹To one another, however, they said: "Truly we are being

to risk losing the only living son of his beloved Rachel. The ten brothers travel together because there is safety in numbers, and perhaps because they hope to secure more rations for the family.

In verse 6 the ten brothers come to Joseph and pay the appropriate homage to him. They bow low just as his boyhood dream predicted. Joseph recognizes them immediately, but does not identify himself to them. On the contrary, he treats them harshly, remembering his dreams and their mocking reaction to them. His accusation that they are spies is plausible because the route into Egypt from Canaan was vulnerable to attack. In their effort to convince him that they are not spies they begin to give him information about the family. The more they tell him, the more he persists in his accusation: his memories of their abuse urge him to be harsh, while his eagerness for news of his father and brother presses him to learn as much as possible from his brothers.

His solution is to impose a series of tests; the first of these is for one brother to go home and bring the youngest while the others wait in prison for them to return. Three days later he changes his orders, sending all of

punished because of our brother. We saw the anguish of his heart when he pleaded with us, yet we would not listen. That is why this anguish has now come upon us." ²²Then Reuben responded, "Did I not tell you, 'Do no wrong to the boy'? But you would not listen! Now comes the reckoning for his blood." ²³They did not know, of course, that Joseph understood what they said, since he spoke with them through an interpreter. ²⁴But turning away from them, he wept. When he was able to speak to them again, he took Simeon from among them and bound him before their eyes. ²⁵Then Joseph gave orders to have their containers filled with grain, their money replaced in each one's sack, and provisions given them for their journey. After this had been done for them, ²⁶they loaded their donkeys with the grain and departed.

²⁷At the night encampment, when one of them opened his bag to give his donkey some fodder, he saw his money there in the mouth of his bag. ²⁸He cried out to his brothers, "My money has been returned! Here it is in my bag!" At that their hearts sank. Trembling, they asked one another, "What is this that God has done to us?"

²⁹When they got back to their father Jacob in the land of Canaan, they told him all that had happened to them. ³⁰"The man who is lord of the land," they said, "spoke to us harshly and put us in custody on the grounds that we were spying on the land. ³¹But we said to him: 'We are honest men; we have never been spies. ³²We are twelve brothers, sons of the same father; but one is no more, and the youngest one is now with our father in the land of Canaan.' ³³Then the man who is lord of the land said to us: 'This

---

them home with food for their families. In this way he assures himself that Jacob and Benjamin will not go hungry. The brothers, still in Joseph's presence, interpret his orders as punishment for their earlier abusive treatment of him, but they do not recognize him.

Reuben's chastisement of the others in verse 22 touches Joseph: he realizes that Reuben tried to save him from the brothers' plot. He leaves the room rather than weep in their presence and divulge his identity. Joseph takes the second-oldest, Simeon, hostage rather than Reuben, the oldest, in light of Reuben's earlier efforts to save him. He arranges for the others to have grain, money, and provisions for the return trip; then the brothers begin their journey home.

They are unaware that their money has been returned until one of them opens his bag and finds it (v. 28). Then the brothers realize that their situation is extremely precarious: they must eventually return to Egypt with their brother Benjamin in order to rescue Simeon and procure more grain, but they risk being accused of stealing the money once they arrive there. The brothers find themselves at the mercy of God in their predicament. Joseph's

is how I will know if you are honest men: leave one of your brothers with me, then take grain for your starving families and go. ³⁴When you bring me your youngest brother, and I know that you are not spies but honest men, I will restore your brother to you, and you may move about freely in the land.'"

³⁵When they were emptying their sacks, there in each one's sack was his moneybag! At the sight of their moneybags, they and their father were afraid. ³⁶Their father Jacob said to them: "Must you make me childless? Joseph is no more, Simeon is no more, and now you would take Benjamin away! All these things have happened to me!" ³⁷Then Reuben told his father: "You may kill my own two sons if I do not return him to you! Put him in my care, and I will bring him back to you." ³⁸But Jacob replied: "My son shall not go down with you. Now that his brother is dead, he is the only one left. If some disaster should befall him on the journey you must make, you would send my white head down to Sheol in grief."

43 **The Second Journey to Egypt.** ¹Now the famine in the land grew severe. ²So when they had used up all the grain they had brought from Egypt, their father said to them, "Go back and buy us a little more food." ³But Judah replied: "The man strictly warned us, 'You shall not see me unless your brother is with you.' ⁴If you are willing to let our

reason for ordering the money to be returned is not given: does he mean for the brothers to have the money because it is theirs? Or does he mean to give them grief? Or is he imposing another test on them?

Once back home, the brothers tell their father about their experiences in Egypt. Ironically they report that they called themselves honest men, still not realizing that they were speaking to the brother they tried to destroy. Then they discover that all their money has been returned, not just one person's. Their father is particularly stricken, fearing that he will lose his youngest son Benjamin to Egypt. Even though Reuben suggests that his own two sons could be ransom for Benjamin, Jacob will not agree to let Benjamin go. This is the last time the narrative depicts Reuben taking leadership in his position as firstborn. From now on it is Judah who assumes responsibility for his brothers. Judah is Jacob's fourth son; the first three (Reuben, Simeon, and Levi) have disgraced themselves: Simeon and Levi in the destruction of Shechem in chapter 34, and Reuben by sleeping with his father's concubine in 35:22.

43:1-34 The second journey to Egypt

The family gradually uses all the rations the brothers brought home from Egypt, and Jacob suggests a second trip to buy more food for them. Judah reminds him of the terms: Benjamin must go with them, or they will all be

brother go with us, we will go down to buy food for you. [5]But if you are not willing, we will not go down, because the man told us, 'You shall not see me unless your brother is with you.'" [6]Israel demanded, "Why did you bring this trouble on me by telling the man that you had another brother?" [7]They answered: "The man kept asking about us and our family: 'Is your father still living? Do you have another brother?' We answered him accordingly. How could we know that he would say, 'Bring your brother down here'?"

[8]Then Judah urged his father Israel: "Let the boy go with me, that we may be off and on our way if you and we and our children are to keep from starving to death. [9]I myself will serve as a guarantee for him. You can hold me responsible for him. If I fail to bring him back and set him before you, I will bear the blame before you forever. [10]Had we not delayed, we could have been there and back twice by now!"

[11]Israel their father then told them: "If it must be so, then do this: Put some of the land's best products in your baggage and take them down to the man as gifts: some balm and honey, gum and resin, and pistachios and almonds. [12]Also take double the money along, for you must return the amount that was put back in the mouths of your bags; it may have been a mistake. [13]Take your brother, too, and be off on your way back to the man.

---

condemned as spies. Jacob now realizes how precarious their situation is: the brothers must take Benjamin with them if they return to Egypt. Jacob is distraught that his sons gave the Egyptian official so much information about their family, but they reply that he pressured them into it, and they complied, not knowing how the information would be used against them. Judah pleads with his father that this is their one hope of survival, because only in Egypt will they be able to find food for their families. Judah makes another offer to his father, commenting that they are wasting precious time by debating the inevitable. He pledges that, if the mission fails, he personally will assume the responsibility.

Jacob finally and reluctantly relents in verse 11. He tells his sons to take gifts with them; ironically they include the same items (balm, gum, and resin) the Ishmaelite traders had with them when they bought Joseph from his brothers in 37:25. He also advises them to take double the amount of money that was returned to them, on the chance that it was mistakenly placed in their bags. He sends Benjamin with them as well, calling on the ancient name of God to protect all of them, in the hope that both Benjamin and Simeon will be allowed to return to him. He expresses his own resignation to the possibility of not seeing either of his two sons again. The brothers make the necessary arrangements, taking along twice the amount

[14]May God Almighty grant you mercy in the presence of the man, so that he may let your other brother go, as well as Benjamin. As for me, if I am to suffer bereavement, I shall suffer it."

[15]So the men took those gifts and double the money and Benjamin. They made their way down to Egypt and presented themselves before Joseph. [16]When Joseph saw them and Benjamin, he told his steward, "Take the men into the house, and have an animal slaughtered and prepared, for they are to dine with me at noon." [17]Doing as Joseph had ordered, the steward conducted the men to Joseph's house. [18]But they became apprehensive when they were led to his house. "It must be," they thought, "on account of the money put back in our bags the first time, that we are taken inside—in order to attack us and take our donkeys and seize us as slaves." [19]So they went up to Joseph's steward and talked to him at the entrance of the house. [20]"If you please, sir," they said, "we came down here once before to buy food. [21]But when we arrived at a night's encampment and opened our bags, there was each man's money in the mouth of his bag—our money in the full amount! We have now brought it back. [22]We have brought other money to buy food. We do not know who put our money in our bags." [23]He replied, "Calm down! Do not fear! Your God and the God of your father must have put treasure in your bags for you. As for your money, I received it." With that, he led Simeon out to them.

[24]The steward then brought the men inside Joseph's house. He gave them water to wash their feet, and gave fodder to their donkeys. [25]Then they set out their gifts to await Joseph's arrival at noon, for they had heard that they were to dine there. [26]When Joseph came home, they presented him with the gifts they had brought inside, while they bowed down before him to the ground. [27]After inquiring how they were, he asked them,

of money they owed for the first provisions, and taking their brother Benjamin with them.

In verse 15 the brothers arrive in Joseph's house. When he sees Benjamin with them, he arranges a banquet. His steward makes the arrangements and brings the brothers into the house for the banquet, but they suspect a trap. The narrative describes the reason for their fright: they expect to be enslaved as punishment for stealing the money. In an effort to forestall what they fear is inevitable they immediately explain to the chief steward that they did not, in fact, steal the money on their first trip to Egypt, but it was put back into their bags without their knowing. The chief steward then assures them they have nothing to fear; their God is behind what happened. He then brings their brother Simeon to them and treats the brothers hospitably while they wait for the arrival of their host.

131

"And how is your aged father, of whom you spoke? Is he still alive?" [28]"Your servant our father is still alive and doing well," they said, as they knelt and bowed down. [29]Then Joseph looked up and saw Benjamin, his brother, the son of his mother. He asked, "Is this your youngest brother, of whom you told me?" Then he said to him, "May God be gracious to you, my son!" [30]With that, Joseph hurried out, for he was so overcome with affection for his brother that he was on the verge of tears. So he went into a private room and wept there.

[31]After washing his face, he reappeared and, now having collected himself, gave the order, "Serve the meal." [32]It was served separately to him, to the brothers, and to the Egyptians who partook of his board. Egyptians may not eat with Hebrews; that is abhorrent to them. [33]When they were seated before him according to their age, from the oldest to the youngest, they looked at one another in amazement; [34]and as portions were brought to them from Joseph's table, Benjamin's portion was five times as large as anyone else's. So they drank freely and made merry with him.

44 **Final Test.** [1]Then Joseph commanded his steward: "Fill the men's bags with as much food as they can carry, and put each man's money in the mouth of his bag. [2]In the mouth of the youngest one's bag put also my silver goblet, together with the money

---

When Joseph comes in, they bow down to him as they did before, and as Joseph's dream predicted. He inquires about their father, using the Hebrew word "shalom" or "wholeness," the expression for health and well-being, in verses 27-28. Joseph then acknowledges Benjamin, but still does not identify himself to his brothers. Then his feelings wash over him, and he leaves the room rather than weep in his brothers' presence. When he returns he orders the meal served. He hosts a feast for his brothers; earlier they enjoyed a meal after throwing him into the cistern (37:25). They are served separately according to the Egyptian custom of not eating with foreigners. (They were considered unclean because they were shepherds.) The brothers are seated according to age, and are amazed at the gracious hospitality of their host. Benjamin receives portions five times larger than the other brothers, but the reason is not given: is Joseph heaping special treatment on his full brother because he is so happy to see him? Or is he watching for signs of envy from his other brothers, like their envy of him when they were young?

44:1-34 The final test

Joseph has still not identified himself to his brothers. He instructs his steward to pack the men's bags with provisions as they prepare to start on their journey home. In addition, the money is to be put back in their bags,

for his grain." The steward did as Joseph said. ³At daybreak the men and their donkeys were sent off. ⁴They had not gone far out of the city when Joseph said to his steward: "Go at once after the men! When you overtake them, say to them, 'Why did you repay good with evil? Why did you steal my silver goblet? ⁵Is it not the very one from which my master drinks and which he uses for divination? What you have done is wrong.'"

⁶When the steward overtook them and repeated these words to them, ⁷they said to him: "Why does my lord say such things? Far be it from your servants to do such a thing! ⁸We even brought back to you from the land of Canaan the money that we found in the mouths of our bags. How could we steal silver or gold from your master's house? ⁹If any of your servants is found to have the goblet, he shall die, and as for the rest of us, we shall become my lord's slaves." ¹⁰But he replied, "Now what you propose is fair enough, but only the one who is found to have it shall become my slave, and the rest of you can go free." ¹¹Then each of them quickly lowered his bag to the ground and opened it; ¹²and when a search was made, starting with the oldest and ending with the youngest, the goblet turned up in Benjamin's bag. ¹³At this, they tore their garments. Then, when each man had loaded his donkey again, they returned to the city.

¹⁴When Judah and his brothers entered Joseph's house, he was still there; so they flung themselves on the ground before him. ¹⁵"How could you do such a thing?" Joseph asked them. "Did you not know that such a man as I could dis-

---

and Joseph's own silver goblet is to be packed in Benjamin's bag. The silver goblet reminds us that the brothers originally sold Joseph for twenty pieces of silver; now he plants a silver vessel in the bag of Benjamin, who had nothing to do with the brothers' earlier abuse of Joseph. His orders are carried out, and early in the morning the party begins the journey home. Very soon after they depart, Joseph sends his steward after the men, to accuse them of stealing the goblet. The steward is not to refer explicitly to the goblet, but only to make an inexact accusation, to heighten the brothers' anxiety.

In verse 7 the brothers are aghast at the steward's accusation. Judah speaks for them all, protesting that they demonstrated their honesty by returning the money and questioning how he could accuse them of stealing something else. He offers to allow the guilty one to be killed, and all the rest of them will become slaves. This spontaneous protestation comes from his own conviction that his brothers are innocent, from the wariness they all experience after the previous incident with the money, and also from his eagerness to resolve the matter as quickly as possible. Judah's response is reminiscent of Jacob's assertion to Laban when he was accused of stealing

cern by divination what happened?" [16]Judah replied: "What can we say to my lord? How can we plead or how try to prove our innocence? God has uncovered your servants' guilt. Here we are, then, the slaves of my lord—the rest of us no less than the one in whose possession the goblet was found." [17]Joseph said, "Far be it from me to act thus! Only the one in whose possession the goblet was found shall become my slave; the rest of you may go back unharmed to your father."

[18]Judah then stepped up to him and said: "I beg you, my lord, let your servant appeal to my lord, and do not become angry with your servant, for you are the equal of Pharaoh. [19]My lord asked his servants, 'Have you a father, or another brother?' [20]So we said to my lord, 'We have an aged father, and a younger brother, the child of his old age. This one's full brother is dead, and since he is the only one by his mother who is left, his father is devoted to him.' [21]Then you told your servants, 'Bring him down to me that I might see him.' [22]We replied to my lord, 'The boy cannot leave his father; his father would die if he left him.' [23]But you told your servants, 'Unless your youngest brother comes down with you, you shall not see me again.' [24]When we returned to your servant my father, we reported to him the words of my lord.

[25]"Later, our father said, 'Go back and buy some food for us.' [26]So we reminded him, 'We cannot go down there; only if our youngest brother is with us can we go, for we may not see the man if our youngest brother is not with us.' [27]Then your servant my father said to us, 'As

the household gods in 31:30-35. But the steward insists that only the guilty one will be enslaved, and no one will be killed.

The brothers open their bags one after another, beginning with the oldest (v. 11). This procedure encourages the brothers, as one bag after another proves not to have the missing vessel. But for the reader, who knows the vessel is in the youngest brother's bag, the suspense mounts as his turn comes closer and closer. When the vessel is found in Benjamin's bag, the brothers are dumbstruck. They tear their clothes, reminiscent of their father's action when he received Joseph's bloodstained garment (37:34). For the third time they go to the city.

When they reach Joseph's house in verse 14, they prostrate themselves again, but this time the narrative uses the intensive form of the verb, expressing the brothers' sense of hopelessness that they will ever be exonerated. Joseph speaks harshly to them, accusing them and wondering how they could do such a thing: do they not realize he knows what happened because of his special powers? Judah, the spokesperson, speaks from the depth of his despair, wondering how the brothers can possibly break free of

you know, my wife bore me two sons. [28]One of them, however, has gone away from me, and I said, "He must have been torn to pieces by wild beasts!" I have not seen him since. [29]If you take this one away from me too, and a disaster befalls him, you will send my white head down to Sheol in grief.'

[30]"So now, if the boy is not with us when I go back to your servant my father, whose very life is bound up with his, he will die as soon as he sees that the boy is missing; [31]and your servants will thus send the white head of your servant our father down to Sheol in grief. [32]Besides, I, your servant, have guaranteed the boy's safety for my father by saying, 'If I fail to bring him back to you, father,

I will bear the blame before you forever.' [33]So now let me, your servant, remain in place of the boy as the slave of my lord, and let the boy go back with his brothers. [34]How could I go back to my father if the boy were not with me? I could not bear to see the anguish that would overcome my father."

45 The Truth Revealed. [1]Joseph could no longer restrain himself in the presence of all his attendants, so he cried out, "Have everyone withdraw from me!" So no one attended him when he made himself known to his brothers. [2]But his sobs were so loud that the Egyptians heard him, and so the news reached Pharaoh's house. [3]"I am Joseph," he said to his brothers. "Is my father still alive?"

the misunderstandings and accusations they have suffered since they first arrived in Egypt. Again he asserts that all the brothers will stand together and accept the punishment of slavery. Joseph insists that only the guilty one will be punished, as his steward had specified.

Then Judah recounts the entire story of the brothers' first arrival in Egypt, the pain and grief their father suffered over the loss of Rachel and over the possible loss of Rachel's only remaining son, the brothers' concern that their father will die of grief if Benjamin does not return to him, and even his own pledge to Jacob that he will assume the guilt if anything happens to Benjamin. With these words Judah brings the story back to its beginning: the one who sold Joseph into slavery is now willing to accept slavery himself rather than devastate their father.

45:1-28 Joseph reveals himself to his brothers

Judah's words touch Joseph so deeply that he can no longer hide his identity from his brothers. He dismisses his attendants, then weeps for the third time. But this time he stays with his brothers, says simply, "I am Joseph," then inquires about his father (45:3). The image of his father's grief over the loss of his two sons by Rachel ultimately moves Joseph to identify himself to his brothers. The brothers are speechless. Joseph repeats

But his brothers could give him no answer, so dumbfounded were they at him.

⁴"Come closer to me," Joseph told his brothers. When they had done so, he said: "I am your brother Joseph, whom you sold into Egypt. ⁵But now do not be distressed, and do not be angry with yourselves for having sold me here. It was really for the sake of saving lives that God sent me here ahead of you. ⁶The famine has been in the land for two years now, and for five more years cultivation will yield no harvest. ⁷God, therefore, sent me on ahead of you to ensure for you a remnant on earth and to save your lives in an extraordinary deliverance. ⁸So it was not really you but God who had me come here; and he has made me a father to Pharaoh, lord of all his household, and ruler over the whole land of Egypt.

⁹"Hurry back, then, to my father and tell him: 'Thus says your son Joseph: God has made me lord of all Egypt; come down to me without delay. ¹⁰You can settle in the region of Goshen, where you will be near me—you and your children and children's children, your flocks and herds, and everything that you own. ¹¹I will provide for you there in the five years of famine that lie ahead, so that you and your household and all that are yours will not suffer want.' ¹²Surely, you can see for yourselves, and Benjamin can see for himself, that it is I who am speaking to you. ¹³Tell my father all about my high position in Egypt and all that you have seen. But hurry and bring my father down here." ¹⁴Then he threw his arms around his brother Benjamin and wept on his shoulder. ¹⁵Joseph then kissed all his brothers and wept over them; and only then were his brothers able to talk with him.

¹⁶The news reached Pharaoh's house: "Joseph's brothers have come." Pharaoh and his officials were pleased. ¹⁷So Pharaoh told Joseph: "Say to your brothers: 'This is what you shall do: Load up your animals and go without delay to the land of Canaan. ¹⁸There get your father and your households, and then come to me; I will assign you the best

---

his identity, adding that he is the one they sold into slavery. His words highlight both his identity and his former strained relationship with them. He then explains that, even though the brothers acted sinfully, everything has happened through God's care, to pave the way for them in Egypt. He sends them back to their father with instructions to bring him back to Egypt, where he will have enough fertile land for his family, livestock, and all his possessions, so they can survive the five years of famine that remain. They will live in Goshen, in the northeastern part of Egypt, where the land is ideal for cattle grazing. Joseph and Benjamin embrace (v. 14), then Joseph embraces each of his other brothers. Finally they are able to talk to him after his shocking revelation, and after all the years of strained relationships (37:15).

land in Egypt, where you will live off the fat of the land.' ¹⁹Instruct them further: 'Do this. Take wagons from the land of Egypt for your children and your wives and bring your father back here. ²⁰Do not be concerned about your belongings, for the best in the whole land of Egypt shall be yours.'"

²¹The sons of Israel acted accordingly. Joseph gave them the wagons, as Pharaoh had ordered, and he supplied them with provisions for the journey. ²²He also gave to each of them a set of clothes, but to Benjamin he gave three hundred shekels of silver and five sets of clothes. ²³Moreover, what he sent to his father was ten donkeys loaded with the finest products of Egypt and another ten loaded with grain and bread and provisions for his father's journey. ²⁴As he sent his brothers on their way, he told them, "Do not quarrel on the way."

²⁵So they went up from Egypt and came to the land of Canaan, to their father Jacob. ²⁶When they told him, "Joseph is still alive—in fact, it is he who is governing all the land of Egypt," he was unmoved, for he did not believe them. ²⁷But when they recounted to him all that Joseph had told them, and when he saw the wagons that Joseph had sent to transport him, the spirit of their father Jacob came to life. ²⁸"Enough," said Israel. "My son Joseph is still alive! I must go and see him before I die."

46 **Migration to Egypt.** ¹Israel set out with all that was his. When he arrived at Beer-sheba, he offered sacrifices to the God of his father Isaac. ²There God, speaking to Israel in a vision by night, called: Jacob! Jacob! He answered, "Here I am." ³Then he said: I am God, the God of your father. Do not be afraid to go down to Egypt, for there I will make you a great nation. ⁴I will go down to Egypt with you and I will also bring you back here, after Joseph has closed your eyes.

In verse 16 Pharaoh himself sends greetings to Joseph's brothers, and encourages Joseph to send for his father and the entire family. He repeats the offer in a formal order. Joseph gives his brothers provisions for their travel; to Benjamin he gives extra gifts, and sends gifts and provisions to his father as well. His final word is puzzling; the Hebrew text can mean, "Do not fear for your safety" or "Do not recriminate."

When Jacob hears that Joseph is not only alive, but a ruler of Egypt, it is his turn to be incredulous (v. 26). When he sees all the provisions Joseph has sent for their journey, he determines to go to Egypt to see Joseph.

46:1–47:12 Jacob's migration to Egypt

Jacob leaves his home, most likely in Hebron (37:14) and goes first to Beer-sheba where he lived with his parents before traveling to Haran (28:10), and where his father Isaac received the Lord's blessing (26:23-25). The connection with Isaac seems to be his reason for going to that place, as the

⁵So Jacob departed from Beer-sheba, and the sons of Israel put their father and their wives and children on the wagons that Pharaoh had sent to transport him. ⁶They took with them their livestock and the possessions they had acquired in the land of Canaan. So Jacob and all his descendants came to Egypt. ⁷His sons and his grandsons, his daughters and his granddaughters—all his descendants—he took with him to Egypt.

⁸These are the names of the Israelites, Jacob and his children, who came to Egypt.

Reuben, Jacob's firstborn, ⁹and the sons of Reuben: Hanoch, Pallu, Hezron, and Carmi. ¹⁰The sons of Simeon: Jemuel, Jamin, Ohad, Jachin, Zohar, and Shaul, son of a Canaanite woman. ¹¹The sons of Levi: Gershon, Kohath, and Merari. ¹²The sons of Judah: Er, Onan, Shelah, Perez, and Zerah—but Er and Onan had died in the land of Canaan; and the sons of Perez were Hezron and Hamul. ¹³The sons of Issachar: Tola, Puah, Jashub, and Shimron. ¹⁴The sons of Zebulun: Sered, Elon, and Jahleel. ¹⁵These were the sons whom Leah bore to Jacob in Paddan-aram, along with his daughter Dinah—thirty-three persons in all, sons and daughters.

¹⁶The sons of Gad: Zephon, Haggi, Shuni, Ezbon, Eri, Arod, and Areli. ¹⁷The sons of Asher: Imnah, Ishvah, Ishvi, and Beriah, with their sister Serah; and the sons of Beriah: Heber and Malchiel. ¹⁸These are the children of Zilpah, whom Laban had given to his daughter Leah; these she bore to Jacob—sixteen persons in all.

¹⁹The sons of Jacob's wife Rachel: Joseph and Benjamin. ²⁰In the land of Egypt Joseph became the father of Manasseh and Ephraim, whom Asenath, daughter of Potiphera, priest of Heliopolis, bore to him. ²¹The sons of Benjamin: Bela, Becher, Ashbel, Gera, Naaman, Ahiram, Shupham, Hupham, and Ard. ²²These are the sons whom Rachel bore to Jacob—fourteen persons in all.

²³The sons of Dan: Hushim. ²⁴The sons of Naphtali: Jahzeel, Guni, Jezer, and Shillem. ²⁵These are the sons of

narrative specifies that he offers sacrifices to "the God of his father Isaac" (v. 1). There he has a vision in which God calls to him and he responds, "Here I am," expressing his readiness to do whatever God asks of him. God reassures him, repeats the promise of a great nation, and promises to bring him back after Joseph closes Jacob's eyes in death. The divine promises provide a clue as to why Jacob visits the shrine: he is leaving this land that has been promised to him, and the future is full of uncertainties. The divine reassurance convinces him that his decision to go to Egypt is a sound one.

It was the custom (and is still so in Jewish families) for the oldest son to close his father's eyes when he dies. Joseph is Jacob's first son by his beloved wife Rachel; here he receives a divine promise that Joseph will be with him at the moment of his death (see 49:33–50:1).

139

Feluccas, Egypt's traditional sailboats, on the Nile River

Bilhah, whom Laban had given to his daughter Rachel; these she bore to Jacob—seven persons in all.

²⁶Jacob's people who came to Egypt—his direct descendants, not counting the wives of Jacob's sons—numbered sixty-six persons in all. ²⁷Together with Joseph's sons who were born to him in Egypt—two persons—all the people comprising the household of Jacob who had come to Egypt amounted to seventy persons in all.

²⁸Israel had sent Judah ahead to Joseph, so that he might meet him in Goshen. On his arrival in the region of Goshen, ²⁹Joseph prepared his chariot and went up to meet his father Israel in Goshen. As soon as Israel made his appearance, Joseph threw his arms around him and wept a long time on his shoulder. ³⁰And Israel said to Joseph, "At last I can die, now that I have seen for myself that you are still alive."

³¹Joseph then said to his brothers and his father's household: "I will go up and inform Pharaoh, telling him: 'My brothers and my father's household, whose home is in the land of Canaan, have come to me. ³²The men are shepherds, having been owners of livestock; and they have brought with them their flocks and herds, as well as everything else they own.' ³³So when Pharaoh summons you and asks what your occupation is, ³⁴you must answer, 'We your servants, like our ancestors, have been owners of livestock from our youth until now,' in order that you may stay in the region of Goshen, since all shepherds are abhorrent to the Egyptians."

A genealogical list follows in verses 8-27, enumerating all those who travel with Jacob to Egypt. The list is arranged according to Jacob's twelve sons and one daughter by their respective mothers. The list includes Er and Onan, Judah's two deceased sons; it also includes Joseph along with his two sons who were born in Egypt. The total number given in verse 26 is sixty-six, not counting Er and Onan, who had already died, or Joseph's two sons who were born in Egypt, or Leah's daughter Dinah, even though she is listed in the genealogy. Then verse 27 gives the number seventy, after adding Joseph's two sons to the count.

Much effort has been made to reconcile these numbers, which have several problematic aspects in addition to the puzzling difference in the totals. For example, the list of Benjamin's sons differs here from corresponding lists in Numbers 26:38-40; 1 Chronicles 7:6; and 8:1-2; each of which is slightly different from the others. Quite possibly the significance of the number seventy, rather than the exact count, is the important aspect of it, as seventy is considered ten times the perfect number seven. (In Exod 1:5, the number of Jacob's family who migrate to Egypt is given as seventy.) The genealogy solemnly testifies that the entire family goes to Egypt, as

47 **Settlement in Goshen.** ¹Joseph went and told Pharaoh, "My father and my brothers have come from the land of Canaan, with their flocks and herds and everything else they own; and they are now in the region of Goshen." ²He then presented to Pharaoh five of his brothers whom he had selected from their full number. ³When Pharaoh asked them, "What is your occupation?" they answered, "We, your servants, like our ancestors, are shepherds. ⁴We have come," they continued, "in order to sojourn in this land, for there is no pasture for your servants' flocks, because the famine has been severe in the land of Canaan. So now please let your servants settle in the region of Goshen." ⁵Pharaoh said to Joseph, "Now that your father and your brothers have come to you, ⁶the land of Egypt is at your disposal; settle your father and brothers in the pick of the land. Let them settle in the region of Goshen. And if you know of capable men among them, put them in charge of my livestock." ⁷Then Joseph brought his father Jacob and presented him to Pharaoh. And Jacob blessed Pharaoh. ⁸Then Pharaoh asked Jacob, "How many years have you lived?" ⁹Jacob replied: "The years I have lived as a wayfarer amount to a hundred and thirty. Few and hard have been these years of my life, and they do not compare with the years that my ancestors lived as wayfarers." ¹⁰Then Jacob blessed Pharaoh and withdrew from his presence.

Genesis 15:13 predicts. The list marks the end of the ancestral period in the land, and provides a transition to the next stage of the family story.

As the party approaches Goshen where they will live, Jacob sends Judah ahead to alert Joseph of their arrival. Thus Judah, who suggested selling Joseph and thus caused his separation from his father, now arranges their reunion. Joseph hurries out to meet his father as the caravan approaches. This time it is he who is overcome; his father expresses his sentiment that now that he has seen Joseph, his life is complete (v. 30). Joseph explains that he will formally notify Pharaoh of his family's arrival, and coaches his brothers that they are to identify themselves as owners of livestock like the Egyptians. This statement is puzzling in view of his final remark, "all shepherds are abhorrent to the Egyptians."

Joseph takes several of his brothers with him when he formally notifies Pharaoh of his family's arrival in 47:1. They state their occupation as shepherds and explain that they have come to stay on a temporary basis because of the famine. Pharaoh gives his formal approval to Joseph, authorizing them to stay in Goshen and serve as royal officers. This designation affords them legal status to which they would not otherwise be entitled as aliens. The approval implicitly makes Joseph responsible for the family.

¹¹Joseph settled his father and brothers and gave them a holding in Egypt on the pick of the land, in the region of Rameses, as Pharaoh had ordered. ¹²And Joseph provided food for his father and brothers and his father's whole household, down to the youngest.

Joseph's Land Policy. ¹³Since there was no food in all the land because of the extreme severity of the famine, and the lands of Egypt and Canaan were languishing from hunger, ¹⁴Joseph gathered in, as payment for the grain that they were buying, all the money that was to be found in Egypt and Canaan, and he put it in Pharaoh's house. ¹⁵When all the money in Egypt and Canaan was spent, all the Egyptians came to Joseph, pleading, "Give us food! Why should we perish in front of you? For our money is gone." ¹⁶"Give me your livestock if your money is gone," replied Joseph. "I will give you food in return for your livestock." ¹⁷So they brought their livestock to Joseph, and he gave them food in exchange for their horses, their flocks of sheep and herds of cattle, and their donkeys. Thus he supplied them with food in exchange for all their livestock in that year. ¹⁸That year ended, and they came to him in the next one and said: "We cannot hide from my lord that, with our money spent and our livestock made over to my lord, there is nothing left to put at my lord's disposal except our bodies and our land. ¹⁹Why should we and our land perish before your very eyes? Take us and our land in exchange for food, and we will become Pharaoh's slaves and our land his property; only

The next audience is between Pharaoh and Jacob (v. 7). Pharaoh asks Jacob about his age, and his reply indicates that he has lived beyond the Egyptian ideal of 110 years. Jacob refers to himself as a wayfarer, perhaps in reference to his life as a journey, perhaps to emphasize his many travels, or perhaps to call attention to his alien status in Egypt. Joseph arranges for his family to have what they need for their stay in Egypt.

47:13-27 Joseph's land policy

The narrative picks up the story from 41:57 when the famine begins to affect everyone. The situation is dire, and Joseph takes drastic steps to keep the people from starving. First he collects all the money in the land as payment for grain, but keeps none of it for himself. Then he barters livestock for grain. When the people have no more livestock they give over their land and become slaves of the state. Thus the state comes to own all the money, livestock, land, and people except for the priests who have a special allotment from Pharaoh. Then Joseph gives the people seed to plant, with the stipulation that they give one-fifth of the crops to Pharaoh at harvest time. The people are profoundly grateful to Joseph, and readily accept the

give us seed, that we may survive and not perish, and that our land may not turn into a waste."

²⁰So Joseph acquired all the land of Egypt for Pharaoh. Each of the Egyptians sold his field, since the famine weighed heavily upon them. Thus the land passed over to Pharaoh, ²¹and the people were reduced to slavery, from one end of Egypt's territory to the other. ²²Only the priests' lands Joseph did not acquire. Since the priests had a fixed allowance from Pharaoh and lived off the allowance Pharaoh had granted them, they did not have to sell their land.

²³Joseph told the people: "Now that I have acquired you and your land for Pharaoh, here is your seed for sowing the land. ²⁴But when the harvest is in, you must give a fifth of it to Pharaoh, while you keep four-fifths as seed for your fields and as food for yourselves and your households and as food for your children." ²⁵"You have saved our lives!" they answered. "We have found favor with my lord; now we will be Pharaoh's slaves." ²⁶Thus Joseph made it a statute for the land of Egypt, which is still in force, that a fifth of its produce should go to Pharaoh. Only the land of the priests did not pass over to Pharaoh.

Joseph Blesses Ephraim and Manasseh. ²⁷Thus Israel settled in the land of Egypt, in the region of Goshen. There they acquired holdings, were fertile, and multiplied greatly. ²⁸Jacob lived in the land of Egypt for seventeen years; the span of his life came to a hundred and forty-seven years. ²⁹When the time

---

terms of the agreement. Meanwhile, Jacob's family thrives in their new home in Egypt (v. 27).

It is difficult to understand this arrangement in contemporary Western terms. In the ancient Near East, during the time of Hammurabi, a tax such as the one Joseph imposed could be as high as two-thirds. In Babylon the rate was between one-fifth and one-third. All these rates seem exorbitant to us; perhaps the narrator thought so, too, and avoided placing the responsibility for the policy on Joseph by having the people suggest enslavement. A brief note follows, that the practice became law, and was still in effect at the time the narrative was written.

By removing any moral stigma from Joseph, the narrative focuses on the wise policies Joseph introduces, portraying him as a concerned and creative administrator who takes bold action in a time of crisis, and thus saves Egypt from devastation.

47:28–48:33 Jacob's last days

When Jacob first arrives in Egypt he rejoices at the opportunity to see Joseph again before he dies; in fact, his sojourn in Egypt extends to seventeen years. This is the same as the amount of time before the two were

approached for Israel to die, he called his son Joseph and said to him: "If it pleases you, put your hand under my thigh as a sign of your enduring fidelity to me; do not bury me in Egypt. ³⁰When I lie down with my ancestors, take me out of Egypt and bury me in their burial place." "I will do as you say," he replied. ³¹But his father demanded, "Swear it to me!" So Joseph swore to him. Then Israel bowed at the head of the bed.

48 ¹Some time afterward, Joseph was informed, "Your father is failing." So he took along with him his two sons, Manasseh and Ephraim. ²When Jacob was told, "Your son Joseph has come to you," Israel rallied his strength and sat up in bed.

³Jacob then said to Joseph: "God Almighty appeared to me at Luz in the land of Canaan, and blessing me, ⁴he said, 'I will make you fertile and multiply you and make you into an assembly of peoples, and I will give this land to your descendants after you as a permanent possession.' ⁵So now your two sons who were born to you in the land of Egypt before I joined you here, shall be mine; Ephraim and Manasseh shall be mine as much as Reuben and Simeon are mine. ⁶Progeny born to you after them shall remain yours; but their heritage shall be recorded in the names of their brothers. ⁷I do this because, when I was returning from Paddan, your mother Rachel died, to my sorrow, during the journey in Canaan, while we were still a short distance from Ephrath; and I buried her there on the way to Ephrath [now Bethlehem]."

⁸When Israel saw Joseph's sons, he asked, "Who are these?" ⁹"They are my sons," Joseph answered his father, "whom God has given me here." "Bring them to me," said his father, "that I may bless them." ¹⁰Now Israel's eyes were

---

separated (37:2), giving a sense of completion to Jacob's sojourn in Egypt. Jacob exacts a solemn oath from Joseph not to bury him in Egypt but to return his remains to the family burial place in the cave of Machpelah. Of all the ancestors, Jacob is the only one to die on alien soil. We can assume from the divine assurance to him at Beer-sheba before leaving for Egypt that Jacob was concerned about leaving the land. The divine promise highlights the importance of his being buried with his forebears in the land promised to him (46:4). Joseph swears to the agreement with the same gesture that Abraham's servant used when he agreed to go to Haran to find a wife for Isaac (24:2-9). Then Jacob bows his head in gratitude, perhaps to Joseph, perhaps to God, or perhaps to both.

Jacob's next act in preparation for death is to establish Joseph's sons as tribes. Joseph receives word in 48:1 that his father is not well. Joseph and his two sons visit his father, who is called Israel here because he is the father, not only of twelve sons, but of twelve tribes. He finds the strength to sit up in bed when his guests arrive. The next few verses are an E variation

dim from age; he could not see well. When Joseph brought his sons close to him, he kissed and embraced them. [11]Then Israel said to Joseph, "I never expected to see your face again, and now God has allowed me to see your descendants as well!"

[12]Joseph removed them from his father's knees and bowed down before him with his face to the ground. [13]Then Joseph took the two, Ephraim with his right hand, to Israel's left, and Manasseh with his left hand, to Israel's right, and brought them up to him. [14]But Israel, crossing his hands, put out his right hand and laid it on the head of Ephraim, although he was the younger, and his left hand on the head of Manasseh, although he was the firstborn. [15]Then he blessed them with these words:

"May the God in whose presence
my fathers Abraham and Isaac
walked,

The God who has been my shepherd
from my birth to this day,
[16]The angel who has delivered me
from all harm,
bless these boys
That in them my name be recalled,
and the names of my fathers,
Abraham and Isaac,
And they may become teeming
multitudes
upon the earth!"

[17]When Joseph saw that his father had laid his right hand on Ephraim's head, this seemed wrong to him; so he took hold of his father's hand, to remove it from Ephraim's head to Manasseh's, [18]saying, "That is not right, father; the other one is the firstborn; lay your right hand on his head!" [19]But his father refused. "I know it, son," he said, "I know. That one too shall become a people, and he too shall be great. Nevertheless, his younger brother shall surpass him, and

on the previous scene. Jacob recalls that at Bethel when he was starting out on his way to Haran (28:18-19), a dream established him as the keeper of the divine promise. Now he formally adopts his two grandsons as his own sons, thus passing the divine promises along to them.

Jacob follows a legal ritual: he formally states his intent to adopt the two boys, asks Joseph to name them, embraces them, and bows profoundly. Verse 6 suggests that Joseph has other sons as well, but Jacob adopts only the first two. Jacob's recollections of Rachel might suggest that she would have had more children if she had lived; but since she died so young Joseph's sons take the place of the children Rachel never had. He highlights his past grief and present joy, commenting that he once thought he would never see his son Joseph again, and now he sees Joseph's children.

Joseph places his sons close to Jacob to receive his blessing, with Manasseh the firstborn in a position to receive the blessing of the firstborn. At this point the text refers to Jacob by his name of Israel, focusing on his role as father of the twelve sons who become the twelve tribes of Israel. He puts

his descendants shall become a multitude of nations." ²⁰So he blessed them that day and said, "By you shall the people of Israel pronounce blessings, saying, 'God make you like Ephraim and Manasseh.'" Thus he placed Ephraim before Manasseh.

²¹Then Israel said to Joseph: "I am about to die. But God will be with you and will restore you to the land of your ancestors. ²²As for me, I give to you, as to the one above his brothers, Shechem, which I captured from the Amorites with my sword and bow."

49 **Jacob's Testament.** ¹Jacob called his sons and said: "Gather around, that I may tell you what is to happen to you in days to come.

²"Assemble and listen, sons of Jacob,
listen to Israel, your father.

³"You, Reuben, my firstborn,
my strength and the first fruit of
my vigor,
excelling in rank and excelling
in power!
⁴Turbulent as water, you shall no
longer excel,

his right hand on the head of his younger grandson Ephraim. Then, before blessing either grandson Israel blesses Joseph, the boys' father. When Joseph tries to reposition Israel's hands so the firstborn will receive the blessing, Israel insists that the younger will be the greater. Thus Israel establishes the younger over the older, just as he received his father Isaac's blessing before Isaac died. The blessing highlights Joseph's privileged place among his brothers, ten of whom are older than he is.

49:1-27 Jacob blesses his sons

Chapter 49 is a complex collection of poems, with sections devoted to each of Jacob's twelve sons. They are arranged in the form of a testament, that is, last words that leave a legacy for his family. Jacob alternates between speaking to the sons and speaking about them; this is awkward for modern readers but was frequent in ancient speech. Jacob first addresses Leah's six sons, then the four sons of the maids, beginning and ending with one of Bilhah's children. Finally he speaks to Joseph and Benjamin, his two youngest sons and his children by his beloved Rachel. Even though he has just adopted Joseph's two sons as his own, they are not included in this testament. In some instances Jacob's words relate to different sons' previous actions; in others the words seem to relate to the lives of the tribes after they settled in the land.

Reuben (vv. 3-4): Jacob voices his condemnation of Reuben for sleeping with Bilhah in 35:22. Historically the tribe of Reuben actually disappeared very early.

for you climbed into your
 father's bed
and defiled my couch to my
 sorrow.

⁵"Simeon and Levi, brothers indeed,
 weapons of violence are their
 knives.
⁶Let not my person enter their
 council,
 or my honor be joined with their
 company;
For in their fury they killed men,
 at their whim they maimed oxen.
⁷Cursed be their fury so fierce,
 and their rage so cruel!
I will scatter them in Jacob,
 disperse them throughout Israel.

⁸"You, Judah, shall your brothers
 praise
 —your hand on the neck of your
 enemies;
 the sons of your father shall
 bow down to you.

⁹Judah is a lion's cub,
 you have grown up on prey,
 my son.
He crouches, lies down like a lion,
 like a lioness—who would dare
 rouse him?
¹⁰The scepter shall never depart from
 Judah,
 or the mace from between his
 feet,
Until tribute comes to him,
 and he receives the people's
 obedience.
¹¹He tethers his donkey to the vine,
 his donkey's foal to the choicest
 stem.
In wine he washes his garments,
 his robe in the blood of grapes.
¹²His eyes are darker than wine,
 and his teeth are whiter than milk.

¹³"Zebulun shall dwell by the
 seashore;
 he will be a haven for ships,
 and his flank shall rest on Sidon.

Simeon and Levi (vv. 5-7): Jacob speaks of the two together, condemning their wanton destruction of the Shechemites in chapter 34, and predicting that they will not remain together. Historically, in time the tribe of Simeon became part of Judah, and the tribe of Levi was given priestly duties rather than land.

Judah (vv. 8-12): After condemning his first three sons for their previous sins, Jacob blesses Judah with the status of firstborn in verse 8b, and assures his authority, especially in verse 10. Historically, Judah remained after the Assyrians destroyed the northern kingdom in 722, bringing to an end the ten tribes who lived in that area.

Zebulun (v. 13): Jacob addresses Zebulun, Leah's sixth son, before her fifth son. Jacob foretells that Zebulun will live by the sea. In fact, his land was inland; perhaps its inhabitants worked along the coast.

Issachar (vv. 14-15): Jacob foresees that this son's tribe will work in servitude.

¹⁴"Issachar is a rawboned donkey,
  crouching between the saddle-
    bags.
¹⁵When he saw how good a settled
    life was,
  and how pleasant the land,
He bent his shoulder to the burden
  and became a toiling serf.

¹⁶"Dan shall achieve justice for his
    people
  as one of the tribes of Israel.
¹⁷Let Dan be a serpent by the road-
    side,
  a horned viper by the path,
That bites the horse's heel,
  so that the rider tumbles back-
    ward.

¹⁸"I long for your deliverance,
  O Lᴏʀᴅ!

¹⁹"Gad shall be raided by raiders,
  but he shall raid at their heels.

²⁰"Asher's produce is rich,
  and he shall furnish delicacies
    for kings.

²¹"Naphtali is a hind let loose,
  which brings forth lovely fawns.

²²"Joseph is a wild colt,
  a wild colt by a spring,
  wild colts on a hillside.
²³Harrying him and shooting,
  the archers opposed him;
²⁴But his bow remained taut,
  and his arms were nimble,
By the power of the Mighty One of
    Jacob,
  because of the Shepherd, the
    Rock of Israel,
²⁵The God of your father, who helps
    you,
  God Almighty, who blesses you,
With the blessings of the heavens
    above,
  the blessings of the abyss that
    crouches below,
The blessings of breasts and womb,
  ²⁶the blessings of fresh grain and
    blossoms,
  the blessings of the everlasting
    mountains,
  the delights of the eternal hills.

Dan (vv. 16-17): Dan, whose name is related to the Hebrew word "judge," will promote justice in his tribe and will fend off his enemies.

A brief prayer for deliverance comes next. In its position after the words about Dan it reinforces the divine source of Dan's ability to judge.

Gad (v. 19): Gad will successfully wage war against his enemies. Historically, his tribe, who lived east of the Jordan River, fought against the other peoples of that area.

Asher (v. 20): Asher inhabited the fertile land along the northwestern coast. It was a rich farming area.

Naphtali (v. 21): The reference to a female, fast-moving animal that bears young is obscure.

Joseph (vv. 22-26): Jacob's words about Joseph, like those about Judah, are lengthy. Parts are obscure; verses 25-26 promise him the blessings of children and land.

May they rest on the head of Joseph,
on the brow of the prince among
his brothers.

27"Benjamin is a ravenous wolf;
mornings he devours the prey,
and evenings he distributes the
spoils."

Farewell and Death. 28All these are the twelve tribes of Israel, and this is what their father said about them, as he blessed them. To each he gave a suitable blessing. 29Then he gave them this charge: "Since I am about to be gathered to my people, bury me with my ancestors in the cave that lies in the field of Ephron the Hittite, 30the cave in the field of Machpelah, facing on Mamre, in the land of Canaan, the field that Abraham bought from Ephron the Hittite for a burial ground. 31There Abraham and his wife Sarah are buried, and so are Isaac and his wife Rebekah, and there, too, I buried Leah—32the field and the cave in it that had been purchased from the Hittites."

33When Jacob had finished giving these instructions to his sons, he drew his feet into the bed, breathed his last, and was gathered to his people.

50 Jacob's Funeral. 1Joseph flung himself upon his father and wept over him as he kissed him. 2Then Joseph ordered the physicians in his service to embalm his father. When the physicians embalmed Israel, 3they spent forty days at it, for that is the full period of embalming; and the Egyptians mourned him for seventy days. 4When the period of mourning was over, Joseph spoke to Pharaoh's household. "If you please, appeal to Pharaoh, saying: 5My father made me swear: 'I am dying. Bury me in my grave that I have prepared for myself in the land of Canaan.' So now let me go up to bury my father. Then I

Benjamin (v. 27): Jacob predicts that this son will be a successful warrior. That depiction does not match the portrayal of the young Benjamin in Genesis. It does, however, address the strategic location of the tribe, dividing the northern tribes from Judah to the south.

49:28–50:14 Jacob's death and burial

After Jacob blesses his sons the story returns to the deathbed scene from 48:22. Jacob's final words repeat the instructions given privately to Joseph, to bury him with his family in the cave of Machpelah (47:29-31). This P version is more formal than the earlier J version. When Jacob dies, Joseph gives instructions for him to be embalmed. This was not the usual ancient Israelite custom, but it preserved Jacob's body so it could be transported back to Hebron as Jacob had requested. The people observe the period of mourning, then carry out Jacob's request, traveling in a large and solemn caravan. After they bury their father the sons all return to Egypt.

will come back." [6]Pharaoh replied, "Go and bury your father, as he made you promise on oath."

[7]So Joseph went up to bury his father; and with him went all of Pharaoh's officials who were senior members of his household and all the other elders of the land of Egypt, [8]as well as Joseph's whole household, his brothers, and his father's household; only their children and their flocks and herds were left in the region of Goshen. [9]Chariots, too, and horsemen went up with him; it was a very imposing retinue.

[10]When they arrived at Goren-ha-atad, which is beyond the Jordan, they held there a very great and solemn memorial service; and Joseph observed seven days of mourning for his father. [11]When the Canaanites who inhabited the land saw the mourning at Goren-ha-atad, they said, "This is a solemn funeral on the part of the Egyptians!" That is why the place was named Abel-mizraim. It is beyond the Jordan.

[12]Thus Jacob's sons did for him as he had instructed them. [13]They carried him to the land of Canaan and buried him in the cave in the field of Machpelah, facing on Mamre, the field that Abraham had bought for a burial ground from Ephron the Hittite.

[14]After Joseph had buried his father he returned to Egypt, together with his brothers and all who had gone up with him for the burial of his father.

Plea for Forgiveness. [15]Now that their father was dead, Joseph's brothers became fearful and thought, "Suppose Joseph has been nursing a grudge against us and now most certainly will pay us back in full for all the wrong we did him!" [16]So they sent to Joseph and said: "Before your father died, he gave us these instructions: [17]'Thus you shall say to Joseph: Please forgive the criminal wrongdoing of your brothers, who treated you harmfully.' So now please forgive the crime that we, the servants of the God of your father, committed."

50:15-26 Final reconciliation

Now that their father is dead, the brothers fear that Joseph will exact revenge for their earlier mistreatment of him. They beg for his forgiveness, and Joseph is moved by their pleading. He answers them in words reminiscent of Jacob's when Rachel begged him for a child (30:2), reminding them that ultimately forgiveness comes from God. Then he sums up the message of the entire Joseph story, pointing out that God uses human actions, no matter how evil or inadequate, to achieve the divine purpose: in this case the survival of Jacob's family.

Then the story jumps ahead to the last days of Joseph, who assures his brothers that God will eventually take them back to the land that has been promised to them. He instructs his brothers to take his body with them when they leave Egypt (Exod 13:19). Joseph, like his father Jacob, is embalmed to preserve his body for its eventual return to the land of promise.

When they said this to him, Joseph broke into tears. [18]Then his brothers also proceeded to fling themselves down before him and said, "We are your slaves!" [19]But Joseph replied to them: "Do not fear. Can I take the place of God? [20]Even though you meant harm to me, God meant it for good, to achieve this present end, the survival of many people. [21]So now, do not fear. I will provide for you and for your children." By thus speaking kindly to them, he reassured them.

[22]Joseph remained in Egypt, together with his father's household. He lived a hundred and ten years. [23]He saw Ephraim's children to the third generation, and the children of Manasseh's son Machir were also born on Joseph's knees.

Death of Joseph. [24]Joseph said to his brothers: "I am about to die. God will surely take care of you and lead you up from this land to the land that he promised on oath to Abraham, Isaac and Jacob." [25]Then, putting the sons of Israel under oath, he continued, "When God thus takes care of you, you must bring my bones up from this place." [26]Joseph died at the age of a hundred and ten. He was embalmed and laid to rest in a coffin in Egypt.

CONCLUSION

Our journey through Genesis began with God's creation of the universe and the first humans, whose early efforts to live in relationship with God and each other formed the basis of life within the human community. The story narrowed its focus from the universal to the family of one couple, Abraham and Sarah. Each time the people took missteps, God took action to reestablish the balance between the divine and human, and within the human community.

Throughout all these events God continued to provide for the peoples' needs. The ancestors were far from perfect or worthy. God guided them, with all their dignity and their frailty, in their comings and goings. Joseph summarized it for his brothers when he pointed out that God uses our actions to achieve the divine end (50:19-20). God continues to use our actions, redeeming what is evil and celebrating what is good. Genesis offers us the models; our lives continue the saga.

REVIEW AIDS AND DISCUSSION TOPICS

Introductory Topics

1. Be familiar with these introductory topics:

   a. The themes of Genesis such as divine causality

   b. Recording the past by storytelling rather than by attention to details in the works

   c. Ancient Near Eastern parallels such as the Mesopotamian creation myth

   d. The documentary theory of J, E, D, P

   e. Ancient literary genres or types of writing (myths, sagas, and genealogies)

   f. The three parts of Genesis

1:1–11:28 The Primeval Story *(pages 11–36)*

1. Compare the two creation stories in Genesis 1 and 2 in terms of the following:

   a. The biblical tradition (J, E, D, or P) of each story

   b. The Creator's name

   c. The original condition of the earth

   d. The time frame for the creation process (how long?)

   e. The creation sequence (what was created first, second, etc.?)

   f. The relationship of humans to the earth

   g. The relationship of man to woman

   h. Overall literary style of each story

2. Access the internet and search for the *Enuma Elish* myth. Note the similarities and differences between this story and the first creation story. What does the myth say about the originality of the Genesis story?

3. Name some of the human conditions and conventions that are explained by the punishment of the serpent, woman, and man.

4. How does God show mercy to the first murderer?

5. List the differences between the J and P versions of the flood story.

6. Access the internet and search for the *Epic of Gilgamesh*. Note the similarities and differences between the epic and the Genesis flood story. What does the epic say about the originality of the Genesis story?

7. What parallel can be drawn from the tower of Babel story and the account of Pentecost in Acts of Apostles 2:1-13?

11:29–25:18 The Ancestral Story, Part 1: Abraham and Sarah
(pages 36–74)

1. Define and describe the term saga.

2. What are the problems connected with the two necessary components of a great nation, namely, children and land? How are these problems solved in the saga of Abraham and Sarah?

3. How would you characterize the marital fidelity of Abraham to Sarah?

4. Read Hebrews 7 and note how the author connects Melchizedek with Jesus Christ.

5. Explain the covenant ritual in Genesis 15:9-21.

6. Review the Hagar and Ishmael story and its significance.

7. A problem among early Christians was the rule, "Unless you are circumcised according to Mosaic practice, you cannot be saved." Read the Acts of the Apostles 15:1-12 to see how this problem is resolved.

8. Be familiar with these stories in this section: a) the three visitors to Abraham, b) Abraham's intercession for Sodom, and c) the birth of Isaac and the banishment of Hagar and Ishmael.

9. Discuss the complexity of Abraham's would-be sacrifice of Isaac in chapter 22. How would you explain this episode?

10. What are the elements of the type scene of the betrothal of Isaac and Rebekah, and where is this type scene repeated in Genesis and Exodus?

25:19–28:9 The Ancestral Story, Part 2: Isaac and Rebekah
(pages 75–84)

1. Identify the various type scenes or motifs that reoccur in this section.

2. What does the sale of Esau's birthright to Jacob tell us about the character of each twin?

3. Review the seven steps in the story of Isaac's blessing of Jacob.

28:10–36:43 The Ancestral Story, Part 3: Jacob and His Wives
(pages 84–109)

1. Be familiar with the elements of Jacob's marriages and the children born of these unions.

2. Review the five stages of the episode of Jacob's taking leave of Laban.

3. How does Jacob receive his new name, Israel?

4. Discuss the moral, political, and economic aspects of the Dinah story.

5. Name the highlights of chapter 35 as this section comes to a close.

37:1–50:26 The Ancestral Story, Part 4: The Joseph Story
(pages 110–150)

1. How does the Joseph story differ from the previous ancestral stories of Genesis?

2. Recount the various dreams of Joseph. Who in the New Testament would qualify as "the master dreamer" (see Matt 1–2)?

3. Review the story of Judah and Tamar (ch. 38).

4. Summarize the highlights of Joseph's experiences in the household of Potiphar, his imprisonment, and his eventual exoneration.

5. Review the comings and goings of Jacob's family into Egypt and their encounters with Joseph.

6. Recount Jacob's final days including the blessing of his sons.

7. How does Joseph reassure his brothers not to fear that he plans to avenge the wrong they did to him?

Conclusion *(page 151)*

1. Discuss some of the major lessons you have learned from this study of Genesis.

2. What sections, incidents, and episodes are most memorable for you in Genesis? What sections are most difficult?

INDEX OF CITATIONS FROM THE
CATECHISM OF THE CATHOLIC CHURCH

The arabic number(s) following the citation refer(s) to the paragraph number(s) in the *Catechism of the Catholic Church*. The asterisk following a paragraph number indicates that the citation has been paraphrased.

Genesis					
1:1–2:4	337	2:17	376,* 396, 400,* 1006,* 1008*	3:17-19	378*
1:1	268,* 279, 280, 290	2:18-25	1605*	3:17	400*
		2:18	371, 1652	3:19	376,* 400, 400,* 1008,* 1609
1:2-3	292*	2:19-20	371, 2417*	3:20	489*
1:2	243,* 703,* 1218*	2:22	369,* 1607*	3:21	1608*
1:3	298*	2:23	371	3:24	332*
1:4	299	2:24	372, 1627,* 1644,* 2335	4:1-2	2335*
1:10	299			4:3-15	401*
1:12	299	2:25	376*	4:3-7	2538*
1:14	347*	3	390,* 2795*	4:4	2569*
1:18	299	3:1-5	391*	4:8-12	2259*
1:21	299	3:1-11	397*	4:10-11	2259
1:26-29	2402*	3:3	1008*	4:10	1736,* 1867,* 2268*
1:26-28	307*	3:5	392, 398,* 399,* 1850	4:25-26	2335
1:26-27	1602*			4:26	2569*
1:26	36,* 225, 299,* 343,*2501, 2809	3:6	2541, 2847	5:1-2	2331
		3:7	400*	5:1	2335*
1:27	355, 383, 1604,* 2331	3:8-10	29*	5:24	2569
		3:9-10	399*	6:3	990*
1:28-31	2415*	3:9	410,* 2568	6:5	401*
1:28	372, 373, 1604, 1607,* 1652, 2331, 2427*	3:11-13	400*	6:9	2569
		3:11	2515	6:12	401*
		3:12	1607*	8:8-12	701*
1:31	299, 1604*	3:13	1736, 2568	8:20-9, 17	2569*
2:1-3	345	3:14-19	2427*	9:1-4	2417*
2:2	314,* 2184	3:15	70,* 410,* 489*	9:5-6	2260
2:7	362, 369,* 703*	3:16-19	1607*	9:8-16	2569*
2:8	378*	3:16	376,* 400,* 1609	9:9	56*
2:15	378	3:16b	1607*		

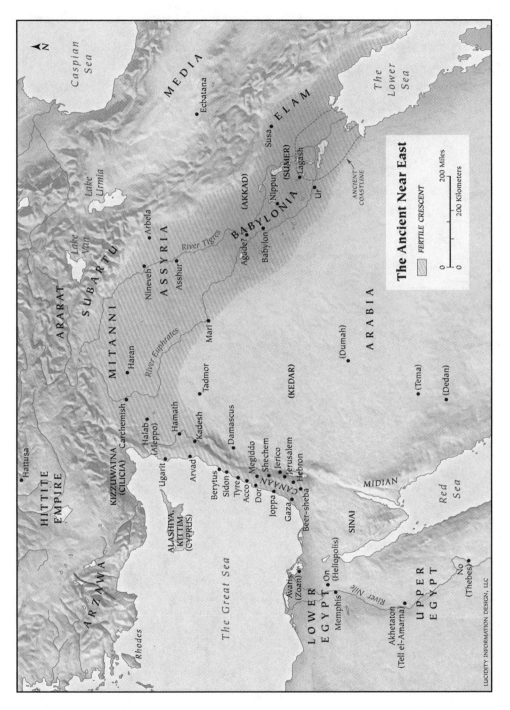

The Ancient Near East

FERTILE CRESCENT

0   200 Miles
0   200 Kilometers

Caspian Sea

MEDIA
• Echatana

ARARAT

SUBARTU

Lake Urmia

Lake Van

ELAM

• Susa

The Lower Sea

MITANNI

ASSYRIA

• Arbela

• Nineveh
• Asshur

River Tigres

Agade? • Babylon

(AKKAD)

BABYLONIA

Nippur •
(SUMER)
Lagash
• Ur

ANCIENT COASTLINE

• Mari

River Euphrates

• Haran

• Tadmor

ARABIA

(Dumah)

(KEDAR)

• Carchemish

• Halab (Aleppo)
• Hamath

KIZZUWATNA (CILICIA)

HITTITE EMPIRE

• Hattusa

ARZAWA

• Kadesh
• Damascus

• Ugarit

Megiddo
Shechem
Jericho
Jerusalem •
• Hebron

• Arvad

CANAAN

Berytus •
Sidon •
Tyre •
Acco •
Dor •

Joppa •
Gaza •
• Beer-sheba

MIDIAN

SINAI

(Tema)

(Dedan)

Red Sea

ALASHIYA, KITTIM (CYPRUS)

The Great Sea

• Rhodes

Avaris (Zoan) •
On (Heliopolis) •

LOWER EGYPT

• Memphis

River Nile

Akhetaton (Tell el-Amarna) •

UPPER EGYPT

No (Thebes) •

LUCIDITY INFORMATION DESIGN, LLC

159

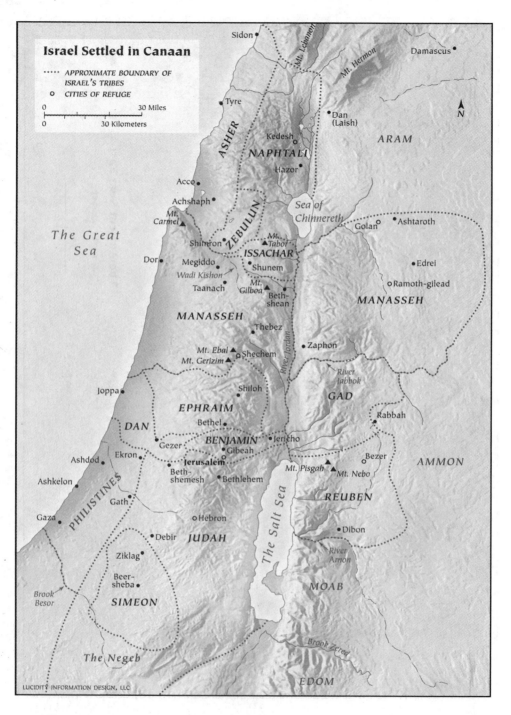

Israel Settled in Canaan

······· APPROXIMATE BOUNDARY OF
ISRAEL'S TRIBES
○   CITIES OF REFUGE

0 ————————— 30 Miles
0 ————————— 30 Kilometers

Sidon

Damascus

Mt. Lebanon

Mt. Hermon

Tyre

Dan
(Laish)

ARAM

Kedesh

ASHER

NAPHTALI

Hazor

Acco

Achshaph

Mt.
Carmel

ZEBULUN

Sea of
Chinnereth

Golan

Ashtaroth

Shimron

Mt.
Tabor

ISSACHAR

*The Great
Sea*

Dor

Megiddo

Shunem

Wadi Kishon

Taanach

Mt.
Gilboa

Beth-
shean

Edrei

Ramoth-gilead

MANASSEH

MANASSEH

Thebez

Zaphon

River Jordan

Mt. Ebal
Mt. Gerizim

Shechem

*River
Jabbok*

Shiloh

GAD

Joppa

EPHRAIM

Bethel

Rabbah

DAN

Gezer

BENJAMIN

Jericho

Bezer

AMMON

Ekron

Gibeah

Ashdod

Jerusalem

Beth-
shemesh

Bethlehem

Mt. Pisgah

Mt. Nebo

Ashkelon

PHILISTINES

REUBEN

Gath

The Salt Sea

Gaza

Hebron

Dibon

Debir

JUDAH

Ziklag

*River
Arnon*

Beer-
sheba

*Brook
Besor*

SIMEON

MOAB

Brook Zered

The Negeb

EDOM

LUCIDITY INFORMATION DESIGN, LLC

160